WHAT PEOPLE ARE SAYING ABOUT

CONTINENTAL REALISM

Paul J. Ennis has given us the first general overview of the theses of After Finitude, and of their reception in the Anglo-American philosophical field. The theses in question – speculative and correlationist – are here exposed with clarity and fidelity. An indispensable introduction to speculative realism.

Professor Quentin Meillassoux, Le Département de philosophie, École normale supérieure

In its brief compass Ennis's book gives a lively, sympathetic though critical account of a newly emergent movement of thought – speculative realism – that looks set to transform received ideas of what counts as "continental" philosophy.

Professor Christopher Norris, Distinguished Research Professor in Philosophy School of English, Communication and Philosophy, Cardiff University

Continental Realism

Paul J. Ennis

Continental Realism

Paul J. Ennis

Winchester, UK
Washington, USA

First published by Zero Books, 2011
Zero Books is an imprint of John Hunt Publishing Ltd., Laurel House, Station Approach,
Alresford, Hants, SO24 9JH, UK
office1@o-books.net
www.o-books.com

For distributor details and how to order please visit the 'Ordering' section on our website.

ISBN: 978 1 84694 719 3

A CIP catalogue record for this book is available from the British Library.

Design: Lee Nash

Printed in the UK by CPI Antony Rowe
Printed in the USA by Offset Paperback Mfrs, Inc

CONTENTS

Preface: The Hermeneutics of the Real

"The real has to be described, not constructed or formed"
Merleau-Ponty[1]

"Hermeneutics is not a privilege of humans but, so to speak, a property of the world itself"
Bruno Latour[2]

Realists, once an unimaginably exotic species among continental philosophers, now roam the continental terrain in abundance. Continental philosophy is no more the vanguard against 'vulgar' and 'naïve' realism, against scientism or against the formal indifference of the other tradition. The prerequisite condition for being a continental philosopher is no longer thinking through the problem of the 'Other' or grasping firmly the secret promise of Hegelianism. In what follows I try to answer a simple question: are we in the midst of a philosophical supersession or not? Is continental philosophy to become continental realism? To answer this question I must first ask if continental realism has yet come face to face with its own limitations. Drawing on recent developments I will show that now, more than ever, the conditions are set for a fruitful division of labour between traditional continental research and realism. What is the task of continental realism in this division of labour? First there is no such thing as continental realism as a method. Further one can no longer accept, as the continental tradition once did, that realism does not intrude upon continental research. Not only does it do so, but it is providing us with a new way to practise our discipline.

Continental realism is a middle path that accepts, contra traditionalist continental philosophy, that the natural sciences, realism, and analytic philosophy are not a threat, but aids in the task of first science: *metaphysics*. Continental realism knows that it does not describe the real, or the 'in-itself,' but it also refuses to partake in the "erosion of the noumena."[3] Continental realism is happy to defer to scientists or mathematicians when it comes to what happens in the real, but we *also* want to hear what metaphysicians have to say. Why not, after all, have many voices trying to articulate the real? Throughout I remain sensitive to the possibility that in exploring realism we may end up occluding what is good in antirealism. We might end up repeating, perhaps unconsciously, the same lop-sidedness that we wanted to overcome. This is also then a meditation on our desire for new beginnings as seen through one particular dilemma: how to think the real as a continental philosopher.

Paul J. Ennis,
Dublin 2010.
ennis.paul@gmail.com

1.1

The Ancestral Realm

The publication of Quentin Meillassoux's short book *After Finitude* has prompted divergent reactions.[4] Alain Badiou, in the preface to *After Finitude,* makes the startling claim that:

> It would be no exaggeration to say that Quentin Meillassoux has opened up a new path in the history of philosophy, hitherto conceived as the history of what it is to know; a path that circumvents Kant's canonical distinction between 'dogmatism', 'scepticism' and 'critique' (AF, vii).

I take Badiou's claim seriously, but there is no denying that Meillassoux's arguments have also prompted numerous critiques. In the first two sections I will argue that what is at stake after Meillassoux is nothing less than the transcendental method itself – the possible supersession of the transcendental tradition, a shift which has no historical precedent save that of phenomenology's total displacement of neo-Kantianism in the early-twentieth century.[5] Meillassoux does not explicitly target transcendentalism, but I think it is possible to show that his principal target is precisely transcendentalism and my immediate task will be to justify this claim. That his critique extends to positions that alter, radicalize or rework the transcendental method cannot change this blunt fact. As Badiou notes Meillassoux's "new path" is opened by circumventing Kant and this is necessary because, as Slavoj Žižek once remarked, "Philosophy as such is Kantian."[6]

The effectiveness of Meillassoux's argument rests on collecting the entire post-Kantian tradition under one simple commitment: "...that there are no objects, no events, no laws, no beings which are not always-already correlated with a point of view, with a subjective access" (TWB, 1).[7] This commitment binds the post-Kantian tradition under the label correlationism. Correlationism is the "...contemporary opponent of any realism" and so, in essence, correlationism is his name for antirealism (TWB, 1). Meillassoux lists three positions that fall under the label of correlationism: transcendentalism, phenomenology and postmodernism.[8] This implies that most correlationists are 'continental' antirealists. These continental antirealist positions tend to emphasize questions of givenness, human access, and transcendental subjectivity.[9] The correlationist claims that when you speak about objects, events, laws or beings you do so in the sense of the correlationist's commitment: *as given*. Meillassoux wants to complicate the correlationist's commitment by introducing an uncorrelated time. He calls this time the *ancestral realm* and he defines it as "...a reality – a thing or event – which existed before life on earth" (TWB, 3). This does not mean that we are unable to discuss the ancestral realm. The empirical sciences do so often, but they resort to indirect means to do so (e.g. radioactive isotopes, or stellar luminescence).

Meillassoux calls the objects that allow us to talk about the ancestral realm *arche-fossils*. In his definition an arche-fossil is "...a material indicating traces of "ancestral" phenomena anterior even to the emergence of life" (TWB, 3). Meillassoux thinks that correlationism can deal with this time, but that an interesting tension arises between correlationism and empirical science based on the correlationist's commitment. One might see what follows as a corrective to this tension rather than a refutation of correlationism.[10] Meillassoux begins *After Finitude* with a short discussion of primary and secondary qualities reminding us that secondary qualities depend on the subjective *relation* between a subject and an object. According to Meillassoux this relational dependence, i.e. that secondary qualities do not subsist outside the relation to a subject, is not problematic. It remains possible to hold the basic Cartesian or Lockean thesis on secondary qualities, "that the sensible *is* a relation," with some alterations to the conception of that relation such that "...it is not particularly difficult for a contemporary philosopher to agree with Descartes or Locke" (AF, 2, his italics). The theory of primary and secondary qualities was not discredited on the basis of secondary qualities, but rather on the distinction between properties that are sensible and those that are in the 'thing-itself':

> For what decisively discredited the distinction between primary and secondary qualities is the very idea of such a distinction: i.e. the assumption that the 'subjectivation' of sensible properties (the emphasis on their essential link to the presence of a subject) could be restricted to the object's sensible determinations, rather than extended to *all* its conceivable properties (AF, 2, his italics).

Meillassoux is sympathetic to the pre-critical commitment to primary qualities – especially the Cartesian claim that primary qualities are mathematical in nature and thereby accessible. Meillassoux intends to revise the Cartesian thesis in a contemporary style allowing him to maintain that "...*all those aspects of the object that can be formulated in mathematical terms can be meaningfully conceived as properties of the object in itself*" (AF, 3, his italics). An immediate problem seems to arise. Such a position seems to reject the Kantian Copernican turn. The Kantian Copernican turn insists that there is no reason *not* to extend the subjectivation of qualities to primary ones. There is a further problem and it relates to how it is that Meillassoux can distinguish between properties found in the relation and those said to exist in the thing-itself. This apparently makes Meillassoux's thesis indefensible because in the post-critical age we know that:

> ...thought cannot get *outside itself* in order to compare the world as it is 'in itself' to the world as it is 'for us,' and thereby distinguish what is a function of our relation to the world from what belongs to the world alone (AF, 3-4, his italics).[11]

It is the 'in-itself' and 'for-us' distinction that now comes to the fore. The act of representing the properties of an 'in-itself' is also the act of making it 'for-us.' Meillassoux teases out the point of departure from 'pre-critical' dogmatic metaphysics toward the 'post-critical' Kantian turn along this distinction. Not only does Kant overturn access to a mind-independent reality, but he inaugurates a reassessment of what a correspondence epistemology might mean. Kantian correspondence does not mean that one's statements directly correspond to a mind-independent object. Rather what is objective is a *representation* that can be universalized and validated on an intersubjective basis.[12] The sum total of these considerations leads Meillassoux to an important conclusion:

> ...the central notion of modern philosophy since Kant seems to be that of *correlation*. By 'correlation' we mean the idea according to which we only ever have access to the correlation between thinking and being, and never to either term considered apart from the other. We will henceforth call *correlationism* any current of thought which maintains the unsurpassable character of the correlation so defined. Consequently, it becomes possible to say that every philosophy which disavows naïve realism has become a variant of correlationism (AF, 5, his italics).

There are three important pieces of information imparted here. The correlationist limits access to what occurs *between* thinking and being. Secondly in order to be a correlationist one must think that this bind is unsurpassable as defined, and finally, in a roundabout sense, that correlationism is a form of antirealism. The correlationist insists that in order to think about subjectivity one must include objectivity and *vice versa*. This is called "the correlationist circle" (AF, 5).[13] More sophisticated forms of correlationism introduce the "correlationist two-step" which asserts the primacy of the *relation* (AF, 5). The two-step emphasizes the 'co' of correlation: "The 'co-' (of co-givenness, of co-relation, of the co-originary, of co-presence, etc.) is the grammatical particle that dominates modern philosophy, its veritable 'chemical formula'" (AF, 5-6). The two twentieth century media of contemporary correlationism are given as consciousness [phenomenology] and language [analytic philosophy] (AF, 7). These mediums function by relativizing content *for us*. For Meillassoux the notion of transcending toward the world is a false image derived from this correlationist relativizing of experience. It masks a loss, and a significant one at that, since this is the loss of:

> ...*the great outdoors*, the *absolute* outside of pre-critical thinkers: that outside which was not relative to us, and which was given as indifferent to its own givenness to be what it is, existing in itself regardless of whether we are thinking of it or not; that outside which thought could explore with the legitimate feeling of being on foreign territory – of being entirely elsewhere (AF, 7 his italics).

The great outdoors is mind-independent, not relative to us, and it is not given *for-us*. But despite this it was once accessible and open to exploration for pre-critical thought. This notion is perhaps the hardest thing for a post-critical philosopher to fathom, and in order to entertain it as a possibility we must once again "...maintain the existence of primary qualities" (AF, 8). Meillassoux tries to evoke a sense of the great outdoors by providing us with a list of statements produced by the empirical sciences:

- The date of the origin of the Universe (13.5 billion years ago)
- The date of the accretion of the earth (4.56 billion years ago)
- The date of the origin of life on earth (3.5 billion years ago)
- The date of the origin of mankind (*Homo habilis,* 2 million years ago) (AF, 9).

These statements are produced by dating various objects and these objects are themselves "...sometimes older than any form of life on earth" (AF, 9). In the nineteen-thirties these dating techniques were perfected and dating became absolute as opposed to relative.[14] Absolute dating allows us, albeit as "revisable hypotheses," to make remarkably determinate statements such as those listed above (AF, 9). Meillassoux is interested in the *meaning* of these statements as they must be interpreted according to the correlationist's commitment:

> How are we to grasp the *meaning* of scientific statements bearing explicitly upon a manifestation of the world that is posited as anterior to the emergence of thought and even of life – *posited, that is, as anterior to every form of human relation to the world?*" (AF, 9-10 his italics)[15]

This question will become more generalized as we proceed, but at this point Meillassoux is interested in how correlationism is "*...liable to interpret these ancestral statements*" (AF, 10 his italics). Meillassoux introduces two types of correlationist thinking. One can posit, from either the transcendental/phenomenological or speculative standpoint, that the correlation cannot be surpassed. Two claims can be made following this positing. The first is that "...all that we can ever apprehend are correlates..." and the second is that "...the correlation as such is eternal" (AF, 10). The latter claim Meillassoux calls the "*hypostasis* of the correlation" and it is not strictly a form of correlationism, but a metaphysics that phenomenalizes all content, including ancestral events, through the eyes of "an attentive God" (AF, 11). The hypostasis of the correlation inscribes into ancestral events an eternal structure thereby dissolving the question Meillassoux has posed.

Correlationism proper does not resort to metaphysics. The correlation itself can be invoked to "curb every hypostatization" (AF, 11). The previous standpoint, which had posited an eternalized correlate, cannot be maintained according to strict correlationism. This is because one cannot get 'around' the correlation in order to verify its truth. Strict correlationism places a limit on metaphysical speculation including speculation *about* the correlation. The guiding question is now refined by Meillassoux as follows: "...once one has situated oneself in the midst of the correlation, while refusing its hypostatization, how is one to interpret an ancestral statement?" (AF, 11). Meillassoux returns briefly to Cartesianism and the primary/secondary quality distinction. How might a physicist, one versed in the Cartesian distinction, interpret ancestral events? In cases where one is discussing an event such as the accretion of the earth secondary qualities do not enter the picture since they belong to the relation between subject and object. But the physicist would argue that we *can* derive meaning from the mathematical data (i.e. the date when the accretion began)

> ...our Cartesian physicist will maintain that those statements about the accretion of the earth which can be mathematically formulated designate actual properties of the event in question (such as its date, its duration, its extension), even when there was no observer present to experience it directly (AF, 12).

These statements will not be considered complete or unrevisable. Falsification is always possible for the physicist, but until a better theory is put forward the scientist will claim that it is sensible to accept the statement as true. In this sense it is easier for the physicist to come to an accommodation with Cartesianism than correlationism. In particular the Cartesian retention of primary mathematical qualities is the definitive factor in making it more amenable to the sciences than correlationism.

By claiming that primary qualities are contingent upon the relation the correlationist complicates the matter, but this does not mean that the correlationist is incapable of accounting for ancestral statements. The interpretation outlined is however inadmissible for the correlationist "...or at least inadmissible so long as it is interpreted *literally*" (AF, 13, his italics). The physicist's position is for the correlationist *necessarily* naive. If the physicist spent too much time focusing on the metaphysical sense of the statement then scientific progress might be impeded. In this sense naive realism helps rather than hinders scientific progress. The philosopher quietly adds a correction to the naive interpretation of scientific statements, but the correction is enough "...to introduce us to another dimension of thought in its relation to being" (AF, 13). Each ancestral statement made by the scientist will be fleshed out to include the appendage: "*for humans*" (AF, 13, his italics).[16] This correction is not designed to refute the scientific sense of the statement, but is generally interpreted by philosophers as allowing the two stances to co-exist: the original realist statement (science) and the antirealist statement (philosophy).[17]

If we make a literal interpretation of an ancestral statement then the scientific realist statement looks to be "*...its ultimate meaning...*" (AF, 14). The statement does not, in such an analysis, require the kind of deepening that correlationism offers. A literal interpretation of an ancestral statement suggests that the realist meaning is its meaning. The correlationist will note that, from their own perspective, this interpretation leaves them with a "tissue of absurdities" (AF, 14). One absurdity in particular helps rather than hinders the correlationist's case: "...that the fossil-matter is the givenness *in the present* of a being that is *anterior* to *givenness*; that is to say, that an arche-fossil manifests an entity's anteriority *vis-á-vis* manifestation" (AF, 14, his italics). The correlationist claims that there is a contradiction implicit in this definition. Being cannot be prior to givenness. Being can only allow the referent to *give* itself as anterior to givenness. If one stops at the claim that 'being gives itself' then one forgets that it gives itself *as* anterior to givenness. By ignoring the second sense I end up assuming that givenness is a general feature of the physical world. I conflate givenness with the thing. This can happen easily because one can imagine the particular being of an entity flitting out of existence, but still retaining a *trace* in some material that is then 'unlocked' by science. The trace, which is contemporaneous with the scientist, does serve an important empirical purpose. However a discussion of givenness will necessitate a deeper inquiry. The ancestral statement is no longer a straightforward statement, but is far more complex than originally imagined. Such a complication requires a reformulation of the ancestral statement: "The present community of scientists has objective reasons to consider that the accretion of the earth preceded the emergence of hominids by x number of years" (AF, 15).

Correlationism *redefines*, mirroring Kantian transcendentalism, objectivity. The guarantor of objectivity is no longer the object and a statement's correspondence to that object. The guarantee now rests with the possibility of universalizing the statement or more precisely making it an intersubjectively true statement. One must no longer interpret the ancestral statement in its literal sense since this leaves aside the problem of givenness. Givenness is the condition for the universalizing potentiality of any given statement. The ancestral statement must be understood as dealing with a fossil-material that exists, and is experimented upon, in the *present*:

> It is then possible to maintain that the statement is true, insofar as it has its basis in an experience which is by right reproducible by anyone (universality of the statement), without believing naively that its truth derives from its adequation to the effective reality of its referent (a world without a givenness of the world) (AF, 16).

This inverts the intuitive temporal sequencing that a literal interpretation invites. The correlationist insight is derived from its insistence that knowledge is created from the standpoint of the present and read back into the past: "This means that we have to carry out a *retrojection of the past on the basis of the present*" (AF, 16, his italics). Correlationism inscribes a counter-sense into the ancestral statement and one that must include the appendage 'for-us'. In response to the literal interpretation the correlationist has been forced to make two decisions: to *double* the meaning of the statement and to carry out a *retrojection* of the past on the basis of the present.

Meillassoux thinks there are two problems that flow from these decisions. He asks again the question about the date of the accretion of the earth. He insists on a direct response to the question: "Did the accretion of the earth happen, *yes or no?*" (AF, 16, his italics). The correlationist is incapable of such a direct answer. On the one hand the answer to this question is 'yes' because the objectivity of the statement is guaranteed by the intersubjective scientific community. On the other hand the correlationist must also answer 'no' because we cannot take the statement in its naive sense as a direct description of its non-correlated referent. This double-response leads to an:

> ...extraordinary claim: *the ancestral statement is a true statement,* in that it is objective, but *one whose referent cannot possibly have actually existed in the way this truth describes it*. It is a true statement, but what it describes as real is an impossible event;

> it is an 'objective' statement, but it has no conceivable object. Or to put it more simply: it is *a non-sense* (AF, 16-17, his italics).

This double-meaning commits correlationism to a *counter-sense* which is an *inverted* sense of the literal interpretation. The literal sense is now subordinate to the *deeper* meaning derived from the correlationist criterion. Further the attendant retrojection that the correlationist imposes on the ancestral statement also "amounts to a *veritable* counter-sense" (AF, 17, his italics). But by removing the realist claim implicit in the original literal interpretation one does not, according to Meillassoux, deepen the interpretation, but rather one has "cancelled" this sense completely (AF, 17). This leads Meillassoux to an important statement about the implications of the correlationist position in relation to ancestral statements:

> This is what we shall express in terms of the ancestral statement's *irremediable* realism: either this statement has a realist sense, and *only* a realist sense, or it has no sense at all. This is why a consistent correlationist should stop 'compromising' with science and stop believing that he can reconcile the two levels of meaning without undermining the content of the scientific statement which he claims to be dealing with. There is no possible compromise between the correlation and the arche-fossil: once one has acknowledged one, one has thereby disqualified the other. (AF, 17, his italics).

These remarks remind us that the correlationist position is by no means innocent. The problem of the ancestral realm seems to force correlationism into a deeply counter-intuitive position. This is not a problem in itself, but it is clear that the correlationist cannot easily come to an easy agreement with science on this issue.[18] The correlationist looks to be, at this point, a full-blown antirealist incapable of accommodating a particular kind of realist statement. Meillassoux is aware that his depiction of correlationism seems to blur important distinctions between the varieties of correlationism. Transcendental idealism and speculative/subjective idealism seem to bleed together as both masking an "extreme idealism" about the ancestral realm (AF, 18). At this point Meillassoux pauses to consider possible responses from the correlationist side. It is in the consideration of these rejoinders that it becomes clear that Meillassoux considers correlationism as transcendentalism. The first rejoinder fixates on Husserlian adumbrations. Problematically Meillassoux includes Husserl under this initial 'idealist' rejoinder. This occludes the more interesting distinction between givenness and realism that marks the Husserlian understanding of perception and it will be necessary for us to expand upon the limited discussion of Husserl as present in *After Finitude*. The second rejoinder relates directly to the fundamental transcendental distinction between the transcendental and empirical levels bringing us into direct contact with Kant and the problem of embodiment. In both cases it will become clear that Meillassoux is operating with the assumption that the correlationist's commitment is, at its core, a transcendentalist commitment.

1.2

The Correlationist Nexus

a. The Transcendentalist Response I: Husserl, Perception, and Adumbrations

The first rejoinder that Meillassoux considers is the idealist rejoinder. The idealist remarks that the ancestral argument is nothing more than a complicated re-imagining of mundane anti-idealism. The idealist locates the core of Meillassoux's critique as the correlationist inability to think about things or events if they are not "...connected to a relation-to-the-world" (i.e. the correlationist's commitment) (AF, 18). The argument, the idealist notes, can just as easily be extended to spatial distance as to temporal ancientness. Distant objects looked at through a telescope might cause one to miss a local event such as a falling vase. Here the distant craters pose no problem for idealism, but the vase goes un-witnessed. This is an old critique of idealism and the idealist reminds Meillassoux that sophisticated idealism has a solution to the problem – namely the "...*lacunary* nature of the given" (AF, 19, his italics). Meillassoux introduces Husserlian adumbrations as an example of sophisticated idealism. Husserlian adumbrations provide for the inclusion of the non-given in and within given perceptual experience. The idealist ends with the remark that "...even the most elementary theory of perception will insist on the fact that the sensible apprehension of an object always occurs against the backdrop of the un-apprehended" (AF, 19).

It is important to flesh out the role that adumbrations play in Husserl's schema. I do not think that Meillassoux's response, which we will see in a moment, is undermined by engaging with this schema, but rather that Meillassoux's inclusion of Husserl among the idealists hides the transcendental direction that adumbrations lead Husserl. This is important because it reveals that even in his discussion of idealism Meillassoux has in mind the much stronger case presented by transcendentalism. Further the defence by adumbration is a distinctly phenomenological contribution to transcendentalism. It is developed relatively early by Husserl and it is essential enough to the reduction to be carried over into Husserl's later work. In the *Crisis* Husserl provides a sustained argument for grounding the objective on an intersubjective basis.[19] This, as we have seen, Meillassoux considers a definitive characteristic of transcendentalism. Husserl is a relatively uncomplicated example of correlationism and he regularly uses the term correlation. The important section '§46' of the *Crisis* is tellingly entitled: "The Universal *a priori* of correlation".[20] The normally restrained Husserl has this to say about the important transcendental accomplishment achieved in this section:

> Ordinarily we notice nothing of the whole subjective character of the manners of exhibiting 'of' the things, but in reflection we recognize with astonishment that essential *correlations* obtain here which are the component parts of a farther-reaching, universal *a priori*.[21]

The adumbrations argument is deployed in Husserl's proto-phenomenological description of perceptual experience, but it is, for Husserl, more important as a hint to the broader phenomenological field he intends to uncover. Husserl recognizes, as did Hegel, that the emphasis on perceptual experience is a naïve, but obvious place to begin: "...involuntarily, we begin with the intentional analysis of perception (purely as perception of its perceived object) and in fact give privileged status thereby to intuitively given bodies."[22]

Husserl is interested in two features of perceptual experience. The first is the problem of how objects are considered as unified despite 'hiding' aspects of themselves and appearing in different configurations.[23] The second is the problem of how our directed attention toward an object translates into an adequate correspondence to that (cognized) object.[24] Husserl explicitly precludes knowing the 'in-itself' from phenomenological investigation: "Cognition is...only *human cognition,* bound up with *human intellectual forms,* and unfit to reach the very nature of things, to reach the things themselves."[25] In his discussion of adumbrations Husserl discovers that a necessary implication of being able to hold a unified object in perceptual experience is the pregiven. This is entailed precisely because there are lacunae in perceptual experience. If one is aware that objects are many-sided and yet one remains capable of distinguishing that object as a single unit then this can only operate on the further assumption that each object is located in a wider unthematized pregiven region that contains its other sides.[26] This world, which operates covertly, must be pregiven if it is not to 'get in the way.'[27] The task of transcendental phenomenology is to thematize this pregiven.[28] Therefore it is important that we recognize that adumbrations are not mere insurance for the idealist against the un-witnessed argument, but, in the Husserlian sense, the path into the wider, unthematized region of the life-world. In other words they are implicated in the transcendental.

Meillassoux responds to the idealist rejoinder by agreeing that the un-witnessed argument "poses no danger to correlationism" (AF, 20).[29] But this was not *his* argument. The problem of the arche-fossil cannot be equated with either spatial distance or temporal ancientness since it designates an event that is prior to givenness as such. The idealist has assumed that Meillassoux is thinking about the problem of temporal distance rather than "anteriority in time" (AF, 20). This difference is the difference between the un-witnessed argument and the not-given argument. The lacunary angle will not suffice as a defence here. Meillassoux insists that the ancestral argument is of a different (temporal) order to the (spatial) un-witnessed argument. It neither addresses spatial distance nor ancient time, but the 'time' that includes the passage of givenness from *"non-being into being"* (AF, 21, his italics). Science uncovers a 'time' that is not only prior to givenness, but indifferent to it. The challenge from the ancestral argument is once again revised, but this time Meillassoux asks how *"science can think a world wherein spatio-temporal givenness itself came into being within a time and a space which preceded every variety of givenness"* (AF, 22, his italics).

b. The Transcendentalist Response II: Kant, Transcendental Subjectivity and Embodiment

Meillassoux is more concerned about the transcendental correlationist rejoinder than the idealist one.[30] The transcendental response deals with the claim that Meillassoux is confusing the empirical and transcendental levels. The split is, according to the transcendentalist, a clear one: the empirical deals with the content of the natural sciences, but the transcendental deals with the *possibility* of science as such:

> You [Meillassoux] proceed as though the transcendental subject...was of the same nature as the physical organ which supports it...you collapse the distinction between the conscious organ which arose within nature and the subject of science which constructs the knowledge of nature (AF, 22).

The distinction can be enforced along ontological lines since the conscious organ is an entity like all other objects, but the transcendental subject cannot be said to exist in the same manner as an entity. It is "rather a set of *conditions*" that allows for scientific knowledge about entities to be possible (AF, 23, his italics). The critique is simply not applicable to the transcendental subject: "The paradox you [Meillassoux] point to arises from crossing two levels of reflection which should never be allowed to cross" (AF, 23).[31] Mirroring Meillassoux's own critique the transcendentalist is claiming that Meillassoux is cancelling out the *sense* of transcendental statements. The form of this transcendental argument is traditional and we can find an early example in Kant's remarks on nature. Kant attributes the order discovered in nature, or the *appearance* of order in nature, to the transcendental subject:

> Thus we ourselves bring into the appearances that order and regularity in them that we call nature, and moreover we would not be able to find it there if we, or the nature of our mind, had not originally put it there (CPR, A125).[32]

Kant is not arguing that nature is nothing 'in-itself', but rather that the order and regularity we attribute to nature is an additional contribution *from our end*. For nature as such may not possess the clean form that we clothe it in, but in order to make sense of nature we must, in some way, formalize it. The formalization of nature occurs for the transcendental subject *a priori*.[33] In each encounter with nature the formalizing process has 'always-already' occurred:

> Categories are concepts that prescribe laws *a priori* to appearances, thus to nature as the sum total of all appearances...and, since they are not derived from nature, and do not follow it as their pattern (for they would otherwise be merely empirical), the question now arises how it is to be conceived that nature must follow them, i.e., how they can determine *a priori* the combination of the manifold of nature without deriving it from the latter (CPR, B163).

Since the form of nature is prescribed *a priori* it is clear that the transcendental subject is not simply impinged upon by nature. Kant provides a convincing solution to the problem of how it is that the mind and world synchronize so well. The solution also provides evidence that the transcendental subject cannot be explained in a purely empirical register.[34]

The transcendental rejoinder is founded on Kant's strong argument for the necessity of spatio-temporal form to all possible experience. This form is not passively received, but contributed by the subject. The arguments of the 'Transcendental Aesthetic' deal with the principles that guide sensible intuition. As is well known the two *pure* forms of sensible intuition are space and time. For Kant space is our outer sense in that it orders what is outside, and time is our inner sense in that it gives coherence to our inner mental states. Space is not something intuited *from* experience but is prior to all general experiences of spatial relations. The many different spaces encountered are but parts of 'one-space.' In this sense space is an *a priori* intuition. Time too comes 'before' our various temporal experiences. Time, properly understood, is also an *a priori* intuition. Together space and time are the *principles* that govern sensible experience. This applies only to sensible experience and it is quite probable that the 'things in themselves' are not governed by these principles, but this we will never know. The transcendental project does not and cannot admit into the discussion definite claims about the nature of things in themselves. This places Meillassoux's project in direct confrontation with a, but not *the,* fundamental principle of transcendentalism.[35]

The transcendentalist's defence is further founded on the status of the transcendental subject as resistant to empirical explanation. This transcendentalist argument can also be further fleshed out. The general *form* of the argument is that one cannot reduce the transcendental subject to the empirical one. There is more contained in the transcendental subject than is contained in the empirical subject. The empirical subject, as an entity like all others, can be said to exist in time or in the 'time of science.' However the transcendental subject is not merely 'in time,' but experiences 'time' *as* temporality. Temporal experience is not a mere succession of points on the arrow of time, but the experiential feeling of having a past, living in the present, and looking to the future. Time might be applied to both empirical and transcendental subject, but temporality can only be applied to the latter. They are therefore, to it bluntly, different. If we do not recognize this difference then we can be accused of conflating the empirical with the transcendental. Here is how Kant draws out the distinction in the first *Critique*:

> Gradually remove from our experiential concept of a body everything that is empirical in it – the colour, the hardness or softness, the weight, even the impenetrability – there still remains the space that was occupied by the body...and you cannot leave that out. Likewise, if you remove from your empirical concept of every object, whether corporeal or incorporeal, all those properties of which experience teaches you, you could still not take from it that by means of which you think of it as a substance or as dependant on a substance...Thus, convinced by the necessity with which this concept presses itself upon you, you must concede that it has its seat in your faculty of cognition *a priori* (CPR, B6).[36]

Meillassoux's response to the transcendental rejoinder begins by accepting that the transcendental subject exists in a different sense from other entities, but he maintains that it still exists in *some sense* in that it "*takes place*" and has a "*point of view*" (AF, 24 his italics). In particular the transcendental subject relies on the body as a 'retro-transcendental' condition that allows for its emergence:

> Granted, the transcendental is the condition for knowledge of bodies, but it is necessary to add that the body is also the condition for the taking place of the transcendental. That the

> transcendental subject has *this* or that body is an empirical matter, but that *it has* a body is a non-empirical condition of its taking place – the body, one could say, is a 'retro-transcendental' condition for the subject of knowledge. We will invoke an established distinction here and say that a subject is *instantiated* rather than *exemplified* by a thinking body (AF, 25 his italics).

Meillassoux turns the Kantian picture on its head. Since the transcendental subject is an embodied subject, and the empirical subject instantiates, although does not exemplify, the transcendental subject then the distinction between a time that affects the empirical and a time (temporality) that affects the transcendental is radically complicated.[37]

There is no doubting that Meillassoux is fundamentally engaged in a critique of transcendentalism and in particular with the lessons of Kant's *Critique of Pure Reason*. What precisely are these lessons? Kant's main aim in the *Critique* is to provide for metaphysics the same certain ground that one finds in the other sciences (in particular physics, mathematics and logic). The crucial difference between Meillassoux and Kant is how each views the limitations of reason. Meillassoux intends to expand the scope of speculation whereas Kant was engaged in an investigation of the limits of reason. His goal was not to solve the antimonies *per se*, but to ask whether they can be answered at all. Despite this we discover a point of similarity in that both thinkers want to uncover metaphysical *principles*. These principles must be found on the 'side of reason' because the problems of metaphysics are not problems of experience. This is their peculiar nature. Because they are problems that do not fall under experience metaphysics must be an *a priori* science. The positive move in Meillassoux's thinking is the assertion that intellectual intuition can access the absolute. Contra Kant, Meillassoux will claim that access to the 'in-itself' is possible, and that it is pure reason that tells us this. How can one think the 'arche-fossil' or the un-correlated 'in-itself' that exists outside 'transcendental time'? It is to this problem that we now turn.

1.3

The Thought of the 'In-Itself'

a. Intellectual Intuition

What has so far preoccupied Meillassoux is correlationism's *relativizing* of content for us. His desired absolute is a thought that could present itself as "non-relative to us" (AF, 28).[38] To access such a thought Meillassoux must find "another relation to the absolute" (AF, 29). Contra dogmatic metaphysics, it will not be an absolutist explanation, but an "*absolutizing* thought" (AF, 34 his italics).[39] The notion of an absolutizing thought is to be retained despite the assumption that an abandonment of metaphysics is taken to entail a correlative abandonment of the absolute.[40] Meillassoux now makes an important distinction and introduces two models of correlationism. Weak correlationism precludes knowledge of the in-itself, but still allows for its 'thinkability.' Strong correlationism, the contemporary model, does not even allow for this limited 'thinkability.' The coordinates of the critique begin to narrow and operate strictly within the correlationist nexus.[41] Meillassoux's method for gaining access to his absolute is to tease out the internal inconsistencies implicit to this nexus. He clarifies the distinction between the models as follows:

> We claimed above that Kantian transcendentalism could be identified with a 'weak' correlationism. Why? The reason is that the Critical philosophy does not prohibit all relation between thought and the absolute. It proscribes any knowledge of the thing-in-itself (any application of the categories to the supersensible), but maintains the thinkability of the in-itself. According to Kant, we know *a priori* that the thing-in-itself is non-contradictory and that it actually exists.

> By way of contrast, the strong model of correlationism maintains not only that it is illegitimate to claim that we can *know* the in-itself, but *also* that it is illegitimate to claim that we can at least *think* it (AF, 35, his italics).

In defence of the last point strong correlationism attacks two forms of 'absolutism'. Strong correlationism is not just antirealist, but also anti-absolutist, but there is an inconsistency in this anti-absolutism that only becomes clear in strong correlationism's refutation of the different types of absolutism. These are realist absolutism, which argues for a mind-independent reality, and idealist absolutism which attempts to absolutize the correlation. In the case of the realist absolute, the strong correlationist can refute it with the correlationist circle. The second is a more complicated case because it claims the circle is *itself* absolute.[42]

In order to refute this form of absolutism the strong correlationist must show that the correlation is contingent, but this leads to the broader thesis of facticity [the "absence of reason for any reality"] (TWB, 8). In looking to facticity the strong correlationist inadvertently admits the possibility that the correlation is not a "necessary component of every reality" (TWB, 8).[43] Meillassoux is not suggesting that this is what strong correlationists routinely argues for, but that if they are truly committed to defeating the idealist absolute then they must do so with the argument from facticity. The strong correlationist admits that one cannot step outside the correlation in order to deduce the reason for the correlation. The correlation is just a fact and there is no *a priori* reason that explains the correlation's existence. Defeating the idealist absolute comes at a heavy price for the strong correlationist. She has been forced to admit the possible contingency of the correlation. This entails that she can think a *non-correlated* possibility.

If we recall this is precisely what Meillassoux has been

seeking. This non-correlated possibility is proof that one can think an 'in-itself' that is not 'for-us.' The restriction upon thinking the 'in-itself' has been liberated by none other than the strong correlationist. In order to properly undermine correlationism Meillassoux intends to radicalize facticity and he will do so by absolutizing *it*.[44] In doing this Meillassoux develops an ontological principle that states nothing else but the absolute necessity of contingency.[45] Its status as a principle distinguishes it from facts, and it is, according to Meillassoux, to be understood as an *eternal* idea: "Contingency and only contingency, is absolutely necessary: facticity, and only facticity, is not factual, but eternal" (TB, 9). The only necessity here is facticity, and this "non-facticity of facticity" is called the *principle of factiality* (TWB, 9). The form of speculative thinking based on this principle is called *factial speculation* (TWB, 9). For Meillassoux absolute facticity is itself a time, but not the 'time of science' or even human temporality. He calls this time "hyper-chaos" or "*surcontingence*" (TWB, 10, his italics). The influence of hyper-chaos extends even to order and disorder: they are from 'its' perspective "equally contingent" (TWB. 10). The development of this principle has rightly raised some eyebrows. It seems a startling departure from our original aim to come to an accommodation with ancestral statements. What *remains* after Meillassoux's jettisoning of metaphysical necessity is the principle of non-contradiction because in order for things to change for no reason whatsoever they must be capable of becoming different for no reason whatsoever and so must be non-contradictory entities. Meillassoux's rationalist will be unfailingly vigilant about attempts to re-establish *any* metaphysical necessity:

> For it is by progressively uncovering new problems, and adequate response to them that we will give life and existence to a *logos* of contingency, which is to say, a reason emancipated from the principle of reason—*a speculative form of the rational* that would no longer be a metaphysical reason (AF,77).

Earlier in *After Finitude* we learned that "*...it is science itself that enjoins us to discover the source of its own absoluteness*" (AF 28, his italics). Looking at the principle of factiality it is hard to know whether it is designed to affirm this imperative or to wake strong correlationism from its dogmatic slumber.[46] It is clear that it is an ontological rather than a scientific principle. It is nonetheless also clear that Meillassoux's principle is not transcendental in nature. We soon discover that Meillassoux, as one has perhaps already suspected, is a *rationalist*: "I'm a rationalist, and reason clearly demonstrates that you can't demonstrate the necessity of laws: so we should just believe reason and accept this point..." (TWB, 10) Meillassoux's rationalism is a pure form of rationalism – arguably he is even a nomological thinker.[47] His principle does not make sense unless one accepts that, contra strong correlationism (phenomenology in particular); it does not deal with the appearances. It does not matter, according to Meillassoux, that the appearances invite us to seek out necessity, but what does matter is that one cannot demonstrate the necessity that manifests in the appearances. The correlationist might remark that Meillassoux has not refuted correlationism, but developed an even more sophisticated version of it. Is it not, after all, thought that determines how Meillassoux must see things? Has he not, in developing his principle, restored the correlationist appendix: *to think something is to think it for a subject*? And what happens to the earlier project of retrieving Cartesian mathematical properties?[48]

The former question will need to wait for a moment, but mathematics makes its return in Meillassoux's introduction of Hume's problem. This is to be considered the second problem of correlationism alongside the original problem of the arche-fossil. In Chapter 4, "Hume's Problem", Meillassoux revives the Humean problem of prediction, induction, and natural laws. For Meillassoux Hume exemplifies the weakness of induction in proving the necessity of natural laws empirically, but he extends the critique to post-Kantian thinking too. They both depend upon probabilistic reasoning meaning that they never get beyond the gambler's bet, or aleatory reasoning, that natural laws will continue to occur as they have. This reasoning is rooted in the human desire for the illusion of stability operative at the level of sensible appearance. Contra this illusion, Meillassoux wants to inscribe his principle of unreason [back] into the 'things themselves': "...we must project unreason into the things themselves, and discover in our grasp of facticity the veritable intellectual intuition of the absolute" (AF, 82). This 'intellectual intuition' is self-relating. There is intuition because the absolutizing thought is derived from the things themselves and it is intellectual because it does not appear to us in the manifest stability of the appearances that things are 'without reason'. The appearances give a false sense of order underpinned by a radical chaos, but we know this only through reason. An important consequence of this is that one must then consider natural laws to be contingent.

This is the Humean *a priori*: "the same cause may actually bring about 'a hundred different events' (and even many more)" (AF, 90).[49] Meillassoux accepts this on the basis of reason alone, and argues that from the strict point of reason, one cannot demonstrate the necessity of causation. But by remaining on 'the side of reason' do we not open ourselves up to an absurdity? If natural laws are in themselves unstable and contingent then why are they stable in experience? Why don't they change and dramatically at that? Here Meillassoux holds that one is often tempted to conflate the two. Because natural laws are stable in the appearances one tends to infer that they are stable in themselves: "the necessitarian inference" (AF, 94). If natural laws could change then they would and they would do so frequently. This is the "frequentialist implication" (AF, 94). Since natural laws do not change in the appearances it is obvious, so the reasoning goes, that they cannot. It is clear to everyone that if anything in our world can be depended on it is that the sun will rise: that it is *necessary* for the sun to rise. Meillassoux retorts that the necessitarian inference is a piece of mathematical probabilistic reasoning.

In games of chance we soundly apply probabilistic reasoning when faced with consistent results. If in a game of chance we consistently gained the same result we would insist that such consistency belies a hidden reason. If we gained the same result all our lives, as we do with natural laws, we naturally assume that there is a necessary reason for this consistency, but this, according to Meillassoux, is an overextension of probabilistic reasoning. It is to move from the consistency of events occurring within the universe to the ascription of consistency to the universe itself. It is to claim that what appears as the manifest stability in appearances must also hold for the 'in-itself' and this is to overstep the bounds of, otherwise sound, probabilistic reasoning. Meillassoux proposes that if one operates in strict accordance with reason then one must abandon aleatory reasoning about natural laws. That is one must abandon, in answering this question, probabilistic reasoning, the necessitarian inference, and the frequentialist implication. What is needed, considering his important thesis regarding the absolute necessity of contingency, is a "*precise condition for the manifest stability of chaos*" because Meillassoux still needs to explain why it is that natural laws appear to be stable (AF, 101, his italics).[50]

Meillassoux's condition is drawn from Cantor, via Badiou, i.e. the transfinite. The deficiency in probabilistic reasoning is that after Cantor numerical totality has been problematized. Probabilistic reasoning assumes that it can operate within a totalized set of conceivable possibilities. Because the set is totalized it becomes possible to think in terms of a regulated set of potential outcomes. It is then further possible to ascertain a regulative rule or law that allows us to predict these outcomes. Contra this reasoning, the transfinite insists that we must 'detotalize' the set of conceivable possibilities. The central thesis here is that it is precisely 'on the side of reason', that is *a priori,* that there is a seemingly limitless amount of possible outcomes in contrast to the limited actual outcomes. Probabilistic reasoning operates by assuming that it can predict the chance of these outcomes because it can quantify the possible outcomes even if these possibilities are infinite. But post-Cantor one can no longer assume this. There will always be a larger possible count.[51] Contra probabilistic reasoning's assumption of quantification within a totality we discover that such totalization is an impossibility.[52] In this move one can then understand how both the absolute contingency that belongs to the 'things themselves' and manifest stability operate without interference. Meillassoux never quite gets around to solving the problem of just why it is that natural laws do remain stable in phenomenal experience and what precisely the relation between the chaotic noumenal and stable phenomenal is, but what is certain is that Meillassoux has ruled out the necessity of natural laws.[53]

b. The Transcendentalist Response III: Hägglund, Gabriel, and Žižek

Has Meillassoux, with his introduction of intellectual intuition, taken the long way around back to correlationism? This is the question we left unanswered in the previous section. Are Meillassoux's radical pre-critical rationalism, his mathematical instincts, and his distaste for the 'truth' of the appearances not merely a de-transcendentalized correlationism? We will attempt to answer these questions by looking at some of the contemporary responses to Meillassoux's anti-correlationism. Martin Hägglund focuses on Meillassoux's problem of the arche-fossil.[54] Hägglund is also interested in complicating the transcendental picture, but his aim is "to *traverse* the texts of transcendental philosophies of time to show that they presuppose the structure of the trace that contradicts them from within."[55] In both we encounter the problem of retro-transcendental conditions or pre-transcendental material.[56] Hägglund claims that the material of the arche-fossil presupposes the arche-trace of time. It is necessary, in order for us to date arche-fossils, that the events that they point to did leave a 'trace.' On the "question of how ancestral time recorded itself" Hägglund claims that Meillassoux "is strangely silent."[57]

It is difficult to know precisely what Hägglund means by 'recording itself' but is it not clear that for Meillassoux ancestral time 'records' itself in the material as mathematical primary properties? This is, after all, the stated aim of his project in its earliest form i.e. to retrieve/revive the thought of these properties. It is these primary qualities, mathematical in content, which we measure in arche-fossils. Hägglund insists on retaining the complications of transcendentalism, and his response to Meillassoux that "the mathematical calculations of ancestral time...depend on the material support of arche-fossils, which *presuppose* the trace structure of time" simply reasserts the primacy of the transcendental as a set of conditions.[58]

Is not this presupposition the transcendentalist's necessary *retrojection* of the past on the basis of the present? Hägglund does not so much refute Meillassoux as revive that which Meillassoux rejects: the counter-meaning necessary for transcendentalism's reconciliation with the 'time of science'. Hägglund's further argument that we must understand the time of science in the sense of succession because it is *articulated* as preceding and exceeding "the existence of thinking/living beings" confirms that he is likely to retain his ultra-transcendentalism in the face of Meillassoux's critique.[59] Hägglund's claim that time itself has a 'trace-structure,' providing us with a link between absolute time and transcendental time, is a reading that transcendentalizes the trace. The arche-fossil is subsumed into the transcendental narrative. One might ask about the other thought: what if the 'trace' had never been articulated? What about the trace 'in-itself' not *as* a trace i.e. as a non-articulated property residing in the thing? The transcendentalist core of Hägglund's response will be a consistent feature of those who engage with Meillassoux's anti-correlationism.

Both Markus Gabriel and Slavoj Žižek have recently argued for a return to German idealism and transcendental subjectivity with an emphasis on its Hegelian and Schellingian variants and they consider Meillassoux a barrier to this task.[60] Markus Gabriel zeroes in on Meillassoux's critique of fideism and the religionizing of reason: "His [Meillassoux] decision to introduce the necessity of contingency is *partly* based on his criticism of the return of religion in our times."[61] Here we should emphasize the 'partly' since *After Finitude* is by no means an *overtly* political text, but it is true that Meillassoux claims that the 'emptiness' at the heart of the Kantian noumenal invites theological speculation.[62] Meillassoux is also clear that his critique of fideism might have other applications: "We thereby grasp that what is at stake in a critique of the de-absolutizing implication...goes beyond that of the legitimation of ancestral statements" (AF, 49). The problem with this emphasis is that Gabriel fails to contextualize the general thrust of Meillassoux's project. The argument that reason has been religionized is not (yet) a political one, but is aimed squarely at certain strands in contemporary continental philosophy that attempt to install in the 'void' of the in-itself crypto-theological notions. His subtle political remarks are not the *core* of his critique, but asides. For Meillassoux fideism "...is merely the *other name* for strong correlationism" (AF, 48 his italics).[63]

It is Žižek who recognizes the core philosophical import of Meillassoux's remarks:

> ...Meillassoux convincingly argues that the recent rise of irrational religious orientations within philosophy...is not a regression to pre-modern times, but a necessary outcome of Western critical reason.[64]

In Žižek's reading Meillassoux acutely teases out the way in which reason, once it had effectively dressed down religion, started to cannibalize itself. Žižek recognizes that Meillassoux's project, of overcoming finitude, remains faithful to the Copernican turn. It is Meillassoux's stated goal, after all, to access the 'in-itself,' and he intends to do so through an engagement with the transcendental tradition: "Meillassoux's aim is to demonstrate – *after* Kant, that is taking into account the Kantian revolution – the possibility of the cognition of the noumenal In-itself."[65] On this point Meillassoux is, according to Žižek, closer to Hegel than he thinks, but fails to notice this because he uncritically adopts the mainstream Hegelian interpretation. In these three transcendentalist responses it is Hägglund and Žižek who recognize the transcendental core of Meillassoux's project, and Gabriel who misses the mark. Meillassoux is not out to argue for the absolute contingency of all situations in fidelity to the event like his mentor Badiou, but wants to retain a transcendental notion (the 'in-itself') *against* the transcendentalist's limitation ('finitude').[66]

Does this now mean that Meillassoux has not only, via his intellectual intuition, reasserted correlationism but also, via his retention of a transcendental notion, found that he is committed to a complicated but still transcendentalist form of correlationism? To answer this question we must turn to the non-transcendentalist responses to Meillassoux's anti-correlationism. First we will look at an important intervention by Peter Gratton that argues for Meillassoux's ability to think both the phenomenal and noumenal *concurrently*. We will then look at a metaphysical approach to objects that articulates both 'ideal' and 'real' aspects of things by eliding the problem of the phenomenal and noumenal distinction. Harman's object oriented ontology proposes that it is language, in particular metaphor, which offers the path of least resistance to the 'things themselves.'

c. The Speculative Response: Gratton and Harman

It is Peter Gratton's reading that best articulates the reasons for Meillassoux's retention of the phenomenal-noumenal split. Gratton, like all the previous respondents, recognizes that "Meillassoux's investigations into the reality of the *in-itself* works methodically from *within* the Kantian split between the noumenal and phenomenal to *le grand dehors*."[67] At this point Meillassoux's debt to transcendentalism ought to be evident. Gratton also accepts that Meillassoux is implicated in correlationism: "...my claim will ultimately be that Meillassoux himself never quite escapes the correlationist circle..."[68] What is missing in the previous accounts is that, in so much as Meillassoux preserves the phenomenal-noumenal distinction, he does so in the sense that both can be articulated with different means. Aleatory reasoning does describe events in phenomenal experience. Probabilistic reasoning is sound for many situations. The 'in-itself,' in its own right, can be described with a different kind of reasoning – one that operates according to axiomatic set-theory. Each side of the split retains (or regains) its specific character: the phenomenal world still manifests stable appearances and the noumenal world remains radically chaotic. The noumenal is not now described in its content. Intellectual intuition can only make minimal claims about the 'in-itself': it exists, and it could be any way. All that is necessary is that there is absolute contingency.[69]

There is no doubting that Meillassoux has prompted an intensive reflection upon correlationism, but as we have seen there remain distinct concerns that he himself remains implicated in both transcendentalism and correlationism. Accepting Gratton's thesis that Meillassoux has opened up the possibility of thinking this distinction in its duality it is worth asking whether one must proceed by way of the distinction at all in order to reach the things themselves. Graham Harman's object oriented philosophy is an example of a metaphysically realist account of objects that outright rejects the correlationist nexus:

> To revive causation in philosophy means to reject the dominance of Kant's Copernican Revolution and its single lonely rift between people and everything else. Although I will claim that real objects do exist beyond human sensual access to them, this should not be confused with Kant's distinction between phenomena and noumena. Whereas Kant's distinction is something endured by humans alone, I hold that one billiard ball hides from another no less than the ball-in-itself hides from humans.[70]

What distinguishes Harman's objects from Meillassoux's mathematical 'in-itself' is that, contra Meillassoux, Harman thinks that one can have more than minimal knowledge of real objects. Unlike Meillassoux's objects of intellectual intuition or 'problematic' arche-fossils Harman's objects are to be conceived as existing, for the most part, entirely of their own accord. Harman's real objects are not merely real in so much as they are mind-independent, but fully-real charged objects. Harman introduces us to the idea of objects that are more than their relations,[71] and he explicates the point in a number of places, but nowhere is his argument more forceful than in his short article "On Vicarious Causation".[72]

Harman begins with Husserlian ideal objects and Heideggerian real objects.[73] The latter are glimpsed, according to Harman's reading, in the tool-analysis, but they are, of course, broadly absent from Heidegger's own concerns: "Heidegger's tool-analysis unwittingly gives us the deepest possible account of the classical rift between substance and relation" (VC, 177). Harman radicalizes Heidegger's thesis that the theoretical attitude is derivative from our practical concern and argues that even in concern one does not illuminate objects in their depths. Harman argues that for the most part we falsely ascribe human notions *into* objects: "We distort when we see, and distort when we use" (VC, 177). The true test of a metaphysical realism about objects is to deduce how objects *must* interact with each other beginning with only the basic, inevitably anthropocentrically inflected, human insight into object-object interaction. This is not a failure in 'purely' seeing objects, or an embargo on reason in the vein of finitude, but simply the starting point of a first science of objects: "When objects fail us, we experience a negation of their accessible contours and become aware that the object exceeds all that we grasp of it" (VC, 177).[74]

Drawing on Husserl Harman accepts that there are ideal objects that belong in the "the space of purest ideality" (VC, 178). Ideal objects, or sensual objects, are objects as they exist in phenomenal experience: "...phenomena are objects nonetheless: in a new, ideal sense" (VC, 178). Unlike real objects the ideal kinds do not have hidden depths. We encounter them directly and they are the objects encountered in perceptual experience. The ideal object can retain more "possible perceptions" [adumbrations] and nonetheless appear as a totality (VC, 178). This is in keeping with the Husserlian claim that in perceptual experience a lacunary element participates in givenness – a position earlier drawn on by Meillassoux's idealist rejoinder. In Harman's metaphysics "real objects never touch directly" (VC, 179). They reside in a background where 'relations' are not constitutive for their existence: "...their causal relations can only be vicarious" (VC, 179). Whatever real objects are they are not to be understood as things that interact. Rather they are better characterized as things that withdraw. They are the objects that hide behind all specific relations.

Why is this necessary? Harman asks us to consider how it is that ideal objects do not meld together in perceptual experience:

> ...why do all the phenomena not instantly fuse together into a single lump? There must be some unknown principle of

> blockage between them. If real objects require vicarious causation, sensual objects endure a buffered causation in which their interactions are partly dammed or stunted" (VC, 179).

Harman reverses the standard understanding of causation such that it occurs on the phenomenal surface, but not in the space of real objects. Harman articulates this point through a traditional reading of Husserlian intentionality, but draws from it radically different conclusions than Husserl. In his reading Husserlian intentionality is "both one and two" (VC, 181). There is both (1) the unified phenomenal whole that is 'wider' than myself and (2) within the whole we have two distinct objects. The two objects reside on the interior of the phenomenal whole. Harman gives us two objects to consider: an 'I' (or a subject) and a 'tree.' The former he considers real and the latter ideal.

In the intentional act the real 'I' is engaging with the sensual profile of the ideal tree. The ideal side of the tree does not inhabit the intention as the 'I' does i.e. by engaging a sensual profile. The other side of the tree, the tree as a real object, opts out by receding behind the relation. The phenomenal whole is also real since it does not depend on the relations it holds together in this particular configuration. We now have a real phenomenal whole, a real 'I,' and an ideal tree. The latter two inhabit the phenomenal whole on its 'inside.' There is also the real tree receding behind the relation.[75] Harman thinks this real tree exists outside the relation, but still manages to "...affect it along avenues still unknown" (VC, 182).[76] Harman further claims that there are three features of causation. It is vicarious, asymmetrical, and buffered (VC, 184). Causation is buffered when it stops two objects from melding together, it is asymmetrical when it occurs between real and sensual objects, and it is vicarious when it occurs between real objects. In vicarious causation two objects that can never interact directly contact one another indirectly through a meditation that occurs in the ideal realm. In this realm we find asymmetrical causation between sensual and real objects. The sensual object mediates *between* two real objects:

> From the asymmetrical and buffered inner life of an object, vicarious connections arise occasionally (in both senses of the term), giving birth to new objects with their own interior spaces. There is a constant meeting of asymmetrical partners on the interior of some unified object: a real one meeting the sensual vicar or deputy of another. Causation itself occurs when these obstacles are somehow broken or suspended (VC, 185).

The idea is radical, but simple in essence. If one has a phenomenal whole and included in this whole is a real object and an ideal object then these objects are in contact. If one accepts that there are real objects that withdraw from this interaction and nonetheless affect what happens then one must find a way for the real side of the ideal object to communicate with other real objects. For Harman the 'contact point' is the ideal object. But if one is willing to accept this much then how is contact between real objects signalled? Harman introduces the notion of *allure*:

> The separation between a sensual object and its quality can be termed 'allure.' This term pinpoints the bewitching emotional effect that often accompanies this event for humans, and also suggests the related term 'allusion,' since allure merely alludes to the object without making its inner life directly present (VC, 199).

The notion of allure is compared to how metaphor operates – it is not itself to be taken as a metaphor.[77] The explanation is phenomenological in essence: a sensual object cannot be separated from its essential qualities i.e. those fundamental qualities that structure it and make it appear as what it is. But one never encounters this essence directly. If we are sincerely absorbed with a sensual object we are always absorbed by something deeper than these features as they appear. We are also absorbed with its *core*. There is some kind of 'gap' between this core and what attaches to it and it is at this 'gap' that Harman thinks we get vicarious interaction. The potential resting in the core of real objects remains.[78]

What is significant about Harman's reading is that it is an attempt to think *le grand dehors*. What distinguishes his metaphysical realism from Meillassoux's realism is that Harman does not operate 'in and through' transcendentalism or correlationism, but begins from phenomenological experience. Rather than accept the limitations imposed from a strict phenomenological position, in line with the finitude of human reason inherited from transcendentalism, Harman unleashes the speculative scope of reason upon the 'in-itself' by strictly delineating the behaviour of objects from the basic insights of the phenomenological method. In this sense Harman's 'leap' from within phenomenological experience toward the metaphysical 'space' of objects is a hermeneutics of the real. Harman's object oriented ontology is an uncomplicated example of thinking the 'great outdoors.' I have raised Harman in order to show that Meillassoux is not alone in the continental tradition as attempting to think the 'in-itself.' That this attempt has arisen at all is worth investigating and in the following section we will explicate the convergence in recent years of continental realism or metaphysics: the thinking of '*le grand dehors*.'

1.4

Thinking *'le grand dehors'*

a. 'Nature' and the Out-side

If our species has a traditional 'Other' then it is surely 'Nature.' When we say we wish to think the great outdoors then surely we mean we intend to think nature? I read Meillassoux's anti-correlationism as a warning that it is a difficult task to supersede the subtle correlationist assumptions inherited from the transcendental method. This helps to explain the conspicuous absence of post-continental and post-phenomenological thinkers in *After Finitude*, but also why nature remains problematic for us today. We must remember that in his critique Meillassoux never attacks from an external vantage point but simply allows various transcendental positions to draw out their own internal contradictions. In recent years theorists have come to recognize that in relation to Nature correlationist and transcendentalist assumptions abound. Žižek, in particular, has started to undertake a rigorous critique of the concept of Nature.[79] Ecological theorists, such as Daniel B. Botkin, have also argued that not only is the idea of nature as holistic or harmonious an illusion, but that this illusion contributes to rather than helps to solve environmental problems:

> In order to gain a new view, one necessary to deal with global environmental problems, we must break free of old assumptions and old myths about nature and ourselves, while building on the scientific and technical advances of our past.[80]

Included in this critique are theorists who romanticize Nature. One example is the approach of ecocriticism. In his influential *The Song of the Earth*, Jonathon Bate claims that our current situation arises from our "progressive severance from nature."[81] Bate proposes that science could do with a more aesthetic approach to nature. What is necessitated for this to happen is a change in consciousness and he suggests we look to Romantic poetry and Heideggerian dwelling. Why Heidegger? Bate describes Heidegger's later work as a post-phenomenological move toward poetics citing the influence of Hölderlin, Trakl, and Rilke. Poetry's distinct force lies in its autonomy from technological thinking: "...poetry is our way of stepping outside the frame of the technological, of reawakening the momentary wonder of unconcealment."[82] We can get a sense of how different this Heidegger is to that known to philosophers when we reach Devall and Sessions inclusion of Heidegger in their sourcebook for deep ecology. They claim he [Heidegger] "...made three important contributions to the deep, long-range ecology literature."[83] These are summarized as the critique of Western metaphysics since Plato, the task of meditative thinking, and dwelling. There is a further claim that "He [Heidegger] arrived at a bio-centric position in which humans should 'let things be'."[84] I am willing to accept that Heidegger has been influential for deep ecology, but I am certain that this claim requires far more justification than is provided.

Tim Morton argues that 'Nature' is a transcendental ideal. Since 'Nature' as it is 'in-itself' is inaccessible we have filled the void with a symbolic conception of 'Nature'. Try as we might to reach 'Nature' we can never quite get a grip on it. There is, according to Morton, nothing to get a grip on. [85] Nature, in this transcendental-symbolic sense no longer serves its function as a potential retreat or background *from* culture – a true ecology does not recognize the nature-culture distinction. The full implications of this dawning insight are expressed succinctly by Žižek:

> With the latest developments, the discontent shifts from culture to nature itself: nature is no longer 'natural', the

> reliable 'dense' background of our lives; it now appears as a fragile mechanism, which, at any point, can explode in a catastrophic direction.[86]

It is important to note that this is not the (absurd) argument that natural things such as trees, birds, or mountains do not exist or have ceased to exist. What has ceased to exist is the inclusion of them all in a harmonious, interconnected set imbued with pastoral and Romantic notions. This expression of nature includes in itself the necessity of why things happen (the necessitarian inference), but the lesson of our times is exactly the contingency of events in nature. Even human existence can be seen as a contingent outcome, an accident, or an error in its own right:[87]

> Consequently, the important realization to be made, is the one repeatedly argued by Stephen Jay Gould: the utter contingency of our existence. There is no Evolution: catastrophes, broken equilibriums, are all part of natural history; at numerous points in the past, life could have turned towards an entirely different direction. Even the main source of our energy (oil) is the result of a past catastrophe of unimaginable dimensions.[88]

Hence it is increasingly important that we learn to think the 'outside' without conflating this with 'Nature' in the transcendental-symbolic sense. To this end Jane Bennett's vital materialism begins not with the possibility of attunement with a harmonious nature, but rather with becoming attuned to the "strange logic of turbulence" characteristic of the 'outside'.[89] Reaching the more-than-human world requires nothing less than a process of "estrangement."[90] This estrangement evokes the inherent capacity in things that cannot be traced back to human engagement. Since the charge is likely forthcoming it is worth noting that Bennett is aware that this opens her up to the charge of anti-humanism, but this she rejects:

> My claims here are motivated by a self-interested or conative concern for *human* survival and happiness: I want to promote greener forms of human culture and more attentive encounters between people-materialities and thing-materialities.[91]

Bennett's "out-side" cannot help but remind us of Meillassoux's '*le grand dehors*' and the connection extends to her thesis that this outside is comprised of matter, but a "strange dimension of matter".[92] Both insist that, at some point, such an argument must evolve beyond epistemology and become ontology.[93] There remains an interesting problem here. Precisely what is the status of non-human, non-natural things or objects in this schema? If philosophy, after all, has another 'Other' and a more contemporary one at that is it not technics and technical agents? The intersection here between nature/ecology and technology has been defined for some time by Heidegger's thinking, and it is to him that we now turn.

b. '*Wohin haben wir uns verirrt?*'[94]

The question of technics has been dominated for decades by Heidegger's well known analysis of the essence of technology in "The Question of Technology". This lecture is at odds with thinking the great outdoors, but it is important to know why. It is my contention that Heidegger's analysis of the essence of technics is concerned, for the most part, not with technics *per se*, but with the essence of human freedom. In Heidegger's analysis, technics remain ambiguous and obscure. The entire thrust of the argument is that technics cannot be equated with anything technological – in particular not with technological instruments, objects, or apparatuses.[95] Heidegger claims that we think through the question concerning technology via its "instrumental and anthropological definition" ["*die instrumentale und anthropologische Bestummung*" (QCT, 312/8).[96] In his attempt to uncover the conditions for the emergence of the instrumentalist definition Heidegger settles on causation, but this is not causation in the Harmanian sense of the interaction between technical objects, but rather causation as a metaphysical decision of the ancient Greeks. Heidegger does extend causation beyond the human remit in relation to nature. His preferred mode of 'causation' is *poiēsis* (*Her-vor-bringen,* bringing-forth) which he tells us is also characteristic of nature (*physis*). In fact *physis* is "*poiēsis* in the highest sense" ["*Die φύσις ist sogar ποίησις im höchsten Sinne*" (QCT, 317/12).The difference between the natural and the 'unnatural' is that what is brought-forth in nature arises of its own accord, but what is brought forward in technics is brought out by another (from us). But it is precisely when Heidegger shifts the discussion toward the broader epochal significance of technics that we begin to lose sight of technical objects.[97] In Heidegger's etymological discussion of *technē* what is important is that the connection with skilled human activity is both retained and widened to include "the arts of the mind and the fine arts" ["*die hohe Kunst und die schönen Künste*" (QCT, 318/14).[98] The contemporary difference between *poiēsis* and *technē* is, as is well known, severe. Since contemporary technology does not allow things to be brought-forth into appearance it is diagnosed as a "challenging" ["*Herausfordern*"] (QCT, 320/15).

In its epochal sense challenging is Enframing [*das Ge-stell*].[99] What is decisive for Heidegger about Enframing is 'its' capacity to occlude the other path i.e. to set up the conditions for the difficulty of remembering, and thereby retrieving, *poiēsis* as a thought.

This leads to Heidegger's famous proclamation that technology is "*the* danger" ["die *Gefahr*"] (QCT, 331/27 his italics). Here we learn that even the freedom to dominate that belongs to humans is an illusion in and within Enframing. What is lost in our age and never encountered is *our* essence: "*In truth, however, precisely nowhere does man today any longer encounter himself i.e. his essence*" ["*Indessen begegnet der Mensch heute in Wahrheit gerade nirgends mehr sich selber, d.h. seinem Wesen"* (QCT, 332/28). We should remember that this is the precise problematic in Heidegger's reading: the essence of technics is an obstacle to the remembrance of our essence.[100] At the conclusion of the essay the issue of the essence of technics remains unresolved – as ambiguous as ever. In this crucial sense Meillassoux leaves technics ambiguous too. In Meillassoux's discussion of dating techniques we hear almost nothing of the instruments involved.

It is true that Meillassoux zeroes in on the singular force of modern science as the event of Gaileism, but nothing is said about the *event* of technics. Is it not also crucial to the meaning of ancestral statements that they are accessed through sophisticated technical instruments that stand in and extend the human capacity for thought?[101] If we take a sample from Meillassoux's original list of statements, that the Universe is 14 billion years old, it is important to remember the process of ageing the Universe was a combination of mathematical ingenuity *and* technical prowess:

> The measured age of the universe, inferred from Hubble's constant and the measured acceleration, is 14 billion years. There are two completely independent measures of the age of the universe. Radioactive dating via thorium and uranium isotope measurements is applied to the abundances of old halo stars. Both thorium-232, with a half-life of 14 billion years, and uranium-238, with a half-life of 4.5 billion years, have been detected in two halo stars, measured with the *world's largest telescopes*.[102]

If nature has traditionally acted as philosophy's 'other' then it is Stiegler's achievement to show that technics is our 'forgotten other' in the Heideggerian style.[103] Stiegler's "genetic logic" of technical objects is an attempt to discern the retro-transcendental conditions of transcendental subjectivity.[104] The central concern of *Technics and Time* is the disconnection between the proliferation of technics and our relatively weak grasp on technical evolution:

> Today, we need to understand the process of technical evolution given that we are experiencing the deep opacity of contemporary technics; we do not immediately understand what is being played out in technics, nor what is being profoundly transformed therein, even though we unceasingly have to make decision regarding technics, the consequences of which are felt to escape us more and more. And in day to day technical reality, we cannot spontaneously distinguish the long-term processes of transformation from spectacular but fleeting technical innovations.[105]

Whilst one might argue that technology has been extensively treated in relation to the threat it poses to humanity there is very little work that treats the operations of technics and technical objects *on their own terms*.[106] This is a call, on Stiegler's part, for thinkers who can incorporate, rather than reflexively disavow, technics – what Stiegler calls a thinker capable of dealing with the "process of concretization" that one finds in contemporary technical society.[107] Such a task flies in the face of the manifest image which sets itself up against the various dangers that technics is supposed to represent (including rationalism, 'calculation', and even science). Yet contemporary thinking is nowhere if it cannot account, in the strict metaphysical sense, for the basic meaning of the technical object prior to the inevitable political, social, or economic critique that tends to attach itself to discussions of technics from Heidegger on. This feeds back into the artificial memory of the human as somehow always-already having been-there – a memorial time made all the more complicated by the double origin that humans claim. These are the technical one which is already a supplement (a prosthesis) to the basic emergence of the pre-human and the second symbolic one wherein the human comes to reflect on its existence and whose origin rests, presumably, in something more than mere survival or, at the very least, is not only concerned with exteriorization for survival/evolutionary purposes.[108] The latter origin is the source for our manifest image: "This is the real exteriorization, if one can thus express the actual exit from the profoundly natural movement that the technical tendency essentially remains..."[109]

However, in the sense of the establishment of retro-transcendental conditions, Stiegler reminds us that the empirical subject first brought about the 'emergence' of an interior through its engagement with the material world and did so using tools: "...it is rather the evolution of the *what* that has a return effect of the *who* and governs to a certain extent its own differentiation."[110] Intended objects necessitated the emergence of a differentiation between subject and object. Here it might seem that Stiegler's thinking offers a complimentary optimism to Heidegger's deep pessimism[111] on the issue of technics.[112] But Stiegler is equally, if not more, pessimistic on our ability to come to an accommodation to our 'others':

> The increasing intervention of humanity in the course of nature, and by the same token in its own nature, makes it incontestable that humanity's power can reaffirm itself eminently as the power of destruction (of the world) of humanity, and the denaturalization of humanity itself, if it is true that worldness is essential to the human and that the essential characteristics of worldness itself have apparently been destroyed by the technoscientific "world", the germinative body of the human itself having become accessible to technical intervention...[113]

Where have we strayed to? We are beginning to encounter the

coordinates of our contemporary situation: the disenchantment with nature and the distrust of technics. This narrative is intimately tied up with philosophy's final other: the natural sciences. It is to this strained relationship that we now turn in order to better understand the repetitious deficiencies of philosophy is thinking about what is external to it.

1.5

Hegel without Hope

> What would be my...spontaneous attitude toward the universe? It's a very dark one. The first one, the first thesis would have been a kind of total vanity: there is nothing, basically, I mean it quite literally...ultimately there are just some fragments, some vanishing things. If you look at the universe, it's one big void.
> *Žižek*[114]

In the final chapter of *After Finitude,* 'Ptolemy's Revenge,' Meillassoux asks why it is that philosophy alone is incapable of accounting for the temporal discrepancy between thought and being. We might ask an even more direct question: why is it still philosophy that is today incapable of coming to an agreement with nature? The question vexes philosophy for good reasons. After all is this not the meaning of meta-physics? That is to extend beyond nature? Philosophy, both analytic and continental, has also had to defer to the immense success of theoretical physics, cosmology, and astrophysics in providing the wider public with the insights into nature that they desire.[115] This singular explanatory force of modern science is derived, as Meillassoux argues, from its mathematization. It is mathematics that has broadened the range of modern science expanding its own horizon to include meaningful (and revisable hypotheses) that extend beyond immediate experience. In this sense modern science is the *event* of Gaileism. This event allowed assertions about times such as the ancestral realm to "become part of a cognitive process" (AF, 114). That is, this event allowed what can be known about such a time be integrated into science. It also had the effect on culture of revealing the autonomy of the world from us – proving that there existed a world beyond its sensible relation to us, but without mystifying this world.

After the Copernican revolution we are shifted from the centre. Our inheritance is a "glacial" indifferent world "unaffected by our existence or inexistence" (AF, 114). The Galilean-Copernican revolution brings out the thought of thought's contingency. It is then surprising, at least for the non-philosopher, to discover that the Copernican revolution in philosophy (Kant's critical turn) is precisely an inversion of the Copernican turn proper placing the subject firmly at the centre. Meillassoux claims that a more fitting name would be the '*Ptolemaic counter-revolution*' in philosophy (AF, 18). The central contradiction of modern philosophy is that just as the Galilean-Copernican event revealed the possibility of non-correlated knowledge philosophy retreated into a transcendental project that rules out this possibility. The retreat is, I think, best exhibited through Hegel. Hegelian sublation provides the unique means of incorporating into the broader human schema the necessity of error, illusion and contradiction.[116] In turn the inclusion of all three is *necessitated* because sublation is the method that allows Hegel to provide a *genetic* account of Reason's development.[117] Hegel's brilliance lies in showing that the supersession of old truths is not their cancellation *per se*, but their partial retention within new configurations of truth.[118] Hegel has contributed immensely to the phenomenological thesis that even if we are presented with illusion we are also presented with the knowledge that in the past reason has identified illusion and surpassed it.[119] The encounter with doubt, as Merleau-Ponty noted, is coupled with the notion that we can unmask the error as it presents itself to us. Neither doubt nor error can "tear us away from truth."[120] The experience of error is to come into contact with the horizon of truth. This is the Hegelian antidote to the Galilean/Copernican event diagnosed by Badiou as "an almost complete disentanglement of philosophy and mathematics" of which Hegel's contribution was "decisive".[121]

In the *Encyclopaedia Logic* we are told that: "Error or other-being, when superseded, is still a necessary dynamic element of truth: for truth can only be where it makes itself its own result".[122] This description speaks for itself, but I will add the supplement that sublation is, for the most part, future-oriented.[123] This kind of talk cannot help but evoke the tension that belongs to *finitude*: that finite subjects strain their necks toward the infinite.[124] Hegel is differentiated from pre-critical rationalism in that he claims one must not rely on the *intuition* that the 'real is rational'.[125] In so much as Hegel is a rationalist his rationalism rests in his understanding that we are able to conceptualize differences and that there is nothing in the world that cannot be made sense of eventually. What remains unexplained at this point is the 'real is rational/ rational is real' clause. If the future is, in a crucial sense, indeterminate then is it not possible that we will encounter something irrational that resists us? Here I think Hegel's position is nuanced. If we encounter something that partially or even wholly resists our complete knowledge it can still be conceptualized. It cannot escape us making some sense of it – even if that sense is negative i.e. that it is precisely irrational.[126] In turn the lesson of past indeterminacy suggests that the puzzle might yet be solved – sometime in the future when other parts of the puzzle emerge into view.[127] The act of separation between thought and the 'real,' an act achieved by us in reflection, leaves in its wake an unsurpassable gap.[128] We can think this gap in numerous guises: that between mind and matter, empirical and transcendental, subject and object, Dasein and entities, symbolic and real, or human and nature. The gap is the limit of *human finitude*. This is the epistemologist's curse: to be endlessly rebuffed by being, to rail against an unsurpassable limit. The quest after the 'in-itself' seems almost naïve to Hegel: "Hence one can only read with surprise the perpetual remark that we do not know the Thing-in-itself. On the contrary, there is nothing we can know so easily."[129]

German idealism is, *in its very bones,* a dialogue on human freedom. This is its guiding theme. But between Hegel's world and our world lies an insurmountable gap. To think human freedom can no longer be to think the transcendental subject, or to think finitude alone. Our crises are not Hegel's crises and our metaphysical crises do not arise from a grand philosophical dialogue as in German idealism. They emerge from external forces: nature, technics, and science.[130] The latter, in its form as physics, has arguably overtaken philosophy as the first science. From its perspective we might ask how one should think *Spirit* against the backdrop of the final stages of the cosmos:

> ...sooner or later both life and mind will have to reckon with the disintegration of the ultimate horizon, when, roughly one trillion, trillion, trillion (10^{1728}) years from now, the accelerating expansion of the universe will have disintegrated the fabric of matter itself, terminating the possibility of embodiment. Every star in the universe will have burnt out, plunging the cosmos into a state of absolute darkness and leaving behind nothing but spent husks of collapsed matter. All free matter, whether on planetary surfaces or in interstellar space, will have decayed, eradicating any remnants of life based in protons and chemistry, and erasing every vestige of sentience – irrespective of its physical basis. Finally, in a state cosmologists call 'asymptopia', the stellar corpses littering the empty universe will evaporate into a brief hailstorm of elementary particles. Atoms themselves will cease to exist. Only the implacable gravitational expansion will continue, driven by the currently inexplicable force called 'dark energy', which will keep pushing the extinguished universe deeper and deeper into an eternal and unfathomable blackness.[131]

No wonder that Dominic Fox has named our world the 'cold world': a 'disfigured' 'lop-sided' world without "human and metaphysical comfort."[132] This is without getting into financial chaos, war, volcanoes, hurricanes, or oil spills. I am evoking all this because if we are to think Hegel in the cold world then we must undo Hegel's *optimism* and by this we also mean giving up the transcendentalist's claim to the centre ground of the philosophical project. This requires that we recognize that what is irretrievable in Hegel's thinking is *Spirit,* what is irretrievable in transcendentalism is its unreconstructed Ptolemaic stance and that what is irretrievable in continental philosophy is the antirealist assumption. We should aim to think the cold world *without hope.* We must abandon all desire to imbue the world with warmth and all transcendental appeals to finitude and limitation.[133] We should, in turn, regain Hegel's confidence in the *speculative* range of metaphysics: a cold, *dispassionate* metaphysics. The cosmological end, if we look at it as *dispirited* Hegelians, becomes a moment for a renewed speculative project. Our response to the cold world must be a cessation of the fruitless chase after the breadcrumbs of the noumena and the embrace of a transcendentalism without centre. Continental realism promises a new secret Hegelianism: one that sees no limits to its remit, no artificial divisions. It refuses to pay an intellectual tithe. To the proposed question as to whether we are playing out an intellectual supersession or not I answer emphatically that we are. But since the true secret of Hegelianism is the retention of past errors alongside what is now unleashed we do not abolish what has come before. Rather we come to an accommodation, *an accommodation of equals,* in pursuit of the truth of our current situation. That is what it means to be a continental realist.

Footnotes

Preface: The Hermeneutics of the Real

[1] Maurice Merleau-Ponty, *Phenomenology of Perception* trans: Colin Smith (London: Routledge, 2005), xi.

[2] Bruno Latour, *Reassembling the Social: An Introduction to Actor-Network-Theory* (Oxford, Oxford University Press, 2005), 245.

[3] Lee Braver, *A Thing of This World: A History of Continental Anti-Realism* (USA: Northwestern University Press, 2007), 79.

1.1 The Ancestral Realm

[4] Quentin Meillassoux, *Après la finitude: essai sur la nécessité de la contingence* (Paris: Seuil, 2006) translated as Quentin Meillassoux, *After Finitude: An Essay on the Necessity of Contingency* trans. Ray Brassier (London: Continuum, 2008). Hereafter cited as AF referring to the English translation. I will also be referencing a short introductory paper introducing the central ideas of *After Finitude* called "Time without Becoming". http://speculativeheresy.files.wordpress.com/2008/07/3729-time_without_becoming.pdf. This paper was delivered at the Centre for Research in Modern European Philosophy, Middlesex University in May, 2008.Hereafter cited as TWB. It is worth noting that Meillassoux belongs to the group of thinkers known as the speculative realists. My claim that this new path will replace the transcendental method does not refer to speculative realism *per se*, but rather to the broader post-continental trend with its roots in the anti-phenomenological thought of Gilles Deleuze and Alain Badiou. The speculative realists are Quentin Meillassoux, Ray Brassier, Graham Harman, and Iain Hamilton Grant. The label has been heavily critiqued in recent years most notably by its inventor Ray Brassier who notes that: "There is no 'speculative realist' doctrine common to the four of

us: the only thing that unites us is antipathy to what Quentin Meillassoux calls 'correlationism'—the doctrine, especially prevalent among 'Continental' philosophers, that humans and world cannot be conceived in isolation from one other—a 'correlationist' is any philosopher who insists that the human-world correlate is philosophy's sole legitimate concern." Brassier makes this claim in an interview with Bram Ieven for the Dutch magazine nY *Transitzone*: "Against an Aesthetics of Noise": http://www.ny-web.be/transitzone/against-aesthetics-noise.html

[5] See Charles R. Bambach, *Heidegger, Dilthey, and the Crisis of Historicism* (Ithaca and London: Cornell University Press, 1995) and Tom Rockmore, *Heidegger, German Idealism & Neo-Kantianism* (Amherst, NY: Humanity Books, 2000).

[6] Slavoj Žižek, *Organs without Bodies: On Deleuze and Consequences* (New York: Routledge, 2004), 44.

[7] Meillassoux recognises that despite the label correlationist positions are "...extraordinarily varied in themselves" (TWB, 1).

[8] Meillassoux does include analytic philosophy under correlationism in *After Finitude* (AF, 7), but he never provides a complimentary critique of analytic philosophy to mirror the critique of continental correlationism.

[9] One might be inclined to state that not all continental antirealists have givenness as their theme, but Meillassoux's critique is important precisely in that it reveals that, whether it is explicit or not, givenness remains a fundamental commitment of any continental antirealism. In my reading Meillassoux is truly out to critique transcendentalism, or the transcendental method, but he deploys the label correlationist to broaden the *potential* targets of his critique. According to Peter Gratton "Meillassoux's "speculative realism" is dismissive of an entire tradition in post-Kantian French and German phenomenology (Husserl, Sartre, Merleau-Ponty, etc.) and post-phenomenology (Lacan, Derrida, Deleuze, Foucault, etc.)." Peter Gratton, "After the Subject:

Meillassoux's Ontology of 'What May Be'," *Pli: The Warwick Journal of Philosophy* 20 (2009), 60.

[10] Meillassoux concludes the first chapter of *After Finitude* with the following important proviso: "...we should state right away that it is not our aim here to resolve this problem; only to try provide a rigorous formulation of it, and to do so in such a way that its resolution no longer seems utterly inconceivable to us" (AF, 26).

[11] Meillassoux makes it clear that this distinction is the driving force behind his later development of the principle of factiality: "Through this thesis [the principle of factiality], I try to reveal the condition for the thinkability of the fundamental opposition in correlationism, even when this opposition is neither stated nor denied: this is the opposition of the in-itself and the for-us" (TWB, 9).

[12] Meillassoux explains Kant's position as follows: "From this point on, *intersubjectivity*, the consensus of a community, supplants the *adequation* between the representations of a solitary subject and the thing itself as the veritable criterion of objectivity, and of scientific objectivity more particularly. Scientific truth is no longer what conforms to an in-itself supposedly indifferent to the way in which it is given to the subject, but rather what is susceptible of being given as shared by a scientific community" (AF, 4-5, his italics).

[13] Ray Brassier helpfully glosses the meaning of the correlationist circle: "Correlationism is subtle: it never denies that our thoughts or utterances *aim at* or *intend* mind-independent or language-independent realities; it merely stipulates that this apparently independent dimension remains internally related to thought and reality." Ray Brassier, *Nihil Unbound: Enlightenment and Extinction* (London: Palgrave Macmillan, 2007), 51.

[14] Meillassoux describes how these techniques work as follows: "These techniques generally rely upon the constant rate of disintegration of radioactive nuclei, as well as upon the laws of

thermoluminescence – the latter permitting the application of dating techniques to the light emitted from stars" (AF, 9).

[15] It is put more concisely in *Time without Becoming*: "...I ask if correlationism – in any of its versions – is able to give a sense or a meaning to ancestral statements" (TWB, 3). It is worth comparing this to the question put to transcendental phenomenologists by the early phenomenological realist Josef Seifert: "...is human knowledge confined to an immanent sphere of human consciousness and to a world of objects (*noemata*) which derive all their meaning and 'being' from human subjectivity, from man's 'being in the world,' from his transcendental, or even his historical consciousness?" in Josef Seifert, *Back to the Things Themselves* (New York, London: Routledge and Kegan Paul, 1987), 2.

[16] This is a subtle example of the correlationist circle: "Correlationism rests an argument as simple as it is powerful, which can be formulated as follows: there can be no X without a givenness of X, and no theory of X without a positing of X. If you speak about something, the correlationist will say, you speak about something that is given to you, and posited by you" (TWB, 1).

[17] This is the correlationist's affirmation of the "*two levels of meaning*" (AF, 14, his italics).

[18] It is worth noting, as Gratton does, that science has, in its own way, developed its realist dogma: "...Meillassoux is also clear that scientists, for their part, operate from a realist dogmatism that takes for granted that the 'arche-fossil,' the evidence of ancestral events prior to living beings, points without mediation to the 'in-itself' of reality, a realism that Husserl for his part called the 'natural attitude.'" Peter Gratton, "After the Subject: Meillassoux's Ontology of 'What May Be'," *Pli: The Warwick Journal of Philosophy* 20 (2009), 61.

1.2 The Correlationist Nexus

a. The Transcendentalist Response I: Husserl, Perception, and Adumbrations

[19] Edmund Husserl, *The Crisis of European Sciences and Transcendental Philosophy* trans. David Carr (Evanston: Northwestern University Press, 1970).

[20] Ibid., 159.

[21] Ibid., 159, my italics.

[22] Edmund Husserl, *The Crisis of European Sciences and Transcendental Philosophy* trans. David Carr (Evanston: Northwestern University Press, 1970), 160. Regarding Husserl's uncomplicated correlationism it is well known that the phenomenological method does not rely on science as an external condition making Meillassoux's argument internally unproblematic for Husserlian transcendental phenomenology: "...we may use no sort of knowledge arising from the sciences as premises, and we may take the sciences into consideration only as historical facts, taking no position of our own on their truth" Ibid., 147. This is a radical departure from Husserl's earlier position as evidenced in Heidegger's characterization of the young Husserl in *The Hermeneutics of Facticity*: "For Husserl, a definite ideal of science was prescribed in mathematics and the mathematical natural sciences. Mathematics was the model for all scientific disciplines. This scientific ideal came into play in that one attempted to elevate description to the level of mathematical rigor." Martin Heidegger, *Ontology: The Hermeneutics of Facticity* trans. John van Buren. (Bloomington: Indiana University Press, 1999), 56.

[23] Regarding the objects of perceptual experience Merleau-Ponty provides another interesting explanation for this phenomenon of unification. In vision the object remains either at the edges of the visual field or one actively focuses on a particular object. The object at the edge can still be concentrated upon and in focusing one's vision we never exclude the wider visual field.

The shift is one of emphasis or making certain objects dimmer and others sharper. This is the activity of 'sectoring': "In normal vision…I direct my gaze upon a sector of the landscape, which comes to life and is disclosed, while the other objects recede into the periphery and become dormant, while, however, not ceasing to be there." Maurice Merleau-Ponty, *Phenomenology of Perception* trans. Colin Smith (London: Routledge, 2005), 78. This unique ability allows us to maintain the unity of a single object against a background of 'dimmer', unthematized objects. Sartre's contribution to the phenomenology of perception is to focus on the empty 'ground' that allows for the distinguishing of objects. Objects can come to my attention, but none mark the ground itself. They can all slip back into 'what is not at my attention'. They can become indistinguishable. To get a sense of the ground objects must actively 'occupy' it. In the famous case of absence the 'ground' (that is itself nothing) grounds an absence leading to a 'double nihilation' i.e. a nothingness of a ground preparing for an absence, but it is the concrete situation, and not the abstractness of the discourse, that matters here. Sartre wants us to imagine that we really are in a café, to truly expect Pierre to fill this event, and only in this experience can absence be properly understood. Idle musing on absences could play out infinitely, but thinking about absence in terms of an experience reminds us that absence does, in fact, partake in our lives: "The *not*, as an abrupt intuitive discovery, appears as consciousness (of being), consciousness of the *not*." Jean-Paul Sartre, *Being and Nothingness* trans. Hazel E. Barnes (London: Routledge, 1958), 11.

[24] In his own words: "...how can we be certain of the correspondence between cognition and the object cognized? How can knowledge transcend itself and reach its object reliably?" in *Edmund Husserl, The Idea of Phenomenology trans. Lee Hardy (Dordrecht, London: Kluwer Academic, 1999), 15.*

[25] Ibid., 17.

[26] The argument is worth quoting at length: "...there are

various individual things of experience at any given time; I focus on one of them. To perceive it, even if it is perceived as remaining completely unchanged, is something very complex: it is to see it, to touch it, to smell it, to hear it, etc.; and in each case I have something different. What is seen in seeing is in and for itself other than what is touched in touching. But in spite of this I say: it is the same thing; it is only the manners of its sensible exhibition, of course that are different. If I remain purely within the realm of seeing, I find new differences, arising in very manifold form in the course of any normal seeing, which, after all, is a continuous process; each phase is itself a seeing, but actually what is seen in each one is something different...But in them the surface exhibits itself to me in a continuous synthesis; each side is for consciousness a manner of exhibition for it. This implies that, while the surface is immediately given, I mean more than it offers." Edmund Husserl, *The Crisis of European Sciences and Transcendental Philosophy* trans. David Carr (Evanston: Northwestern University Press, 1970), 158.

[27] The more familiar name for this is the life-world: "...the life-world, for us who wakingly live in it, is always already there, existing in advance for us, the 'ground' of all praxis whether theoretical or extratheoretical. The world is pregiven to us, the waking, always somehow interested subjects, not occasionally but always and necessarily as the universal field of all actual and possible praxis, as horizon" (Ibid.,142). Even when the phenomenologist makes it thematic it continues to operate: "...the world, exactly as it was for me earlier and still is, as my world, our world, humanity's world, having validity in its various subjective ways, has not disappeared; it is just that, during the consistently carried-out epoche, it is under our gaze purely as the correlate of the subjectivity which gives it ontic meaning, through whose validities the world 'is' at all" Ibid., 152.

[28] Husserl, at one point, is happy to define transcendental phenomenology as "...a science of the universal how of the

pregivenness of the world..." Ibid., 146.

[29] In defence of Meillassoux we might also point out that it is not strictly necessary that we thematize this Husserlian background. For example John McDowell's *Mind and World* might seem on the surface to deal with traditional transcendentalist themes. Like Husserl, McDowell accepts that perceptual experience entails a pregiven *wider reality*, but, contra Husserl; he does not think it we need to make it thematic. It is enough that we are aware of this wider reality. See John McDowell, *Mind and World* (Cambridge, MA: Harvard University Press, 1994).

b. The Transcendentalist Response II: Kant, Transcendental Subjectivity and Embodiment

[30] Hägglund calls this rejoinder one of Meillassoux's "most ingenious philosophical moves" and recognises that the transcendental subject Meillassoux has in mind here is that of Kant and Husserl. Martin Hägglund, "The Challenge of Radical Atheism: A Response," *CR: The New Centennial Review* 9, no. 1, (2009), 241.

[31] Further to the point: "...you cannot claim your problem is "ontological" rather than empirical, since your problem of the arche-fossil *is* empirical, and only empirical – it pertains to objects. As for the transcendental conditions of cognition, they cannot be said to arise or disappear – not because they are eternal but because they are 'outside time' and 'outside sense' – they remain out of reach of the scientific discourse about objects because they provide the forms for this discourse" (AF, 23, his italics).

[32] References to the *Critique of Pure Reason* (CPR) refer to the Kemp Smith translation: Immanuel Kant, *Critique of Pure Reason* trans. Norman Kemp Smith, New York: St. Martin's Press. 1929.

[33] Kant thinks it is possible to isolate sensibility from the understanding for this particular discussion: "The pure understanding separates itself completely not only from everything

empirical but even from all sensibility. It is therefore a unity that subsists on its own, which is sufficient by itself, and which is not to be supplemented by any external additions" (CPR, A65/B90). The important thing to remember is that in experience both the sensibility and the understanding must be operating in tandem.

[34] Husserl also considers this issue from a more modern perspective in relation to evolution: "Thoughts of a biological order intrude. We are reminded of the modern theory of evolution, according to which man has evolved in the struggle for existence and by natural selection, and with him his intellect too has evolved naturally and along with his intellect all of its characteristic forms, particularly the logical forms." *Edmund Husserl, The Idea of Phenomenology trans. Lee Hardy (Dordrecht, London: Kluwer Academic, 1999), 16.* Husserl does not, of course, deny that the subject is rooted in natural processes and can be conceivably discussed in this way: "To be sure, as with everything else in the world, *cognition*, too, will appear as a problem in a *certain manner*, becoming an object of natural investigation. Cognition is a fact in nature. It is the experience of a cognizing organic being. It is a psychological fact." Ibid., 15, his italics.

[35] Despite the interest it has generated the phenomenal-noumenal distinction is not the core of Kant's project.

[36] It is worth remembering that "...the empirical consciousness that accompanies different representations is by itself dispersed and without relation to the identity of the subject" (CPR, B133). This seems to leave us with a problem, but one that I think has been convincingly explained by John Searle: how does something material such as the brain (the empirical aspect) cause consciousness? And how, in turn, does something immaterial like consciousness engage with the material world? Searle thinks the problem is at least in part linguistic in that we find it difficult to conceptualize how intentional states can be realized in biological systems. The solution for Searle is to de-emphasize 'causation,' in

the philosophical sense of one thing causing another, and rather see it as a case of 'realization.' The mental is realized in the biological *alongside it*. Nor does this mean that subjectivity can be reduced to biology. It is a general fact that each human has their own distinct subjectivity. This is a fact like any other: "...the existence of subjectivity is an objective fact of biology." John Searle, *Minds, Brains, and Science* (Cambridge, MA: Harvard University Press, 1984), 25.

[37] Meillassoux adds that: "We thereby discover that the time of science temporalizes and spatializes the emergence of living bodies; that is to say: *the emergence of the conditions for the taking place of the transcendental*" (AF, 25, his italics).

The Thought of the 'In-Itself'

a. Intellectual Intuition

[38] It ought to be remembered that Meillassoux is ultimately concerned with "thought's relation to the absolute" (AF, 1). Despite opening with the problem of the arche-fossil the bulk of the argument in *After Finitude* is a positive one asserting that it is possible to think a non-correlated absolute.

[39] In the sense of positing an "absolutely necessary being" [real necessity] leading to the thesis that "...every entity is absolutely necessary" [the principle of sufficient reason] (AF, 33).

[40] Meillassoux calls this the "the de-absolutizing implication" (AF, 34)

[41] By correlationist nexus I mean the historical unfolding of the *transcendental method* and the increasing sophistication of transcendentalism as a model for thought. But as a warning it is also important to remember that Meillassoux is not attempting a direct refutation of correlationism, but a reassessment: "...the problem of ancestrality is not – not at all – intended as a refutation of correlationism. In fact, in the first chapter of *After Finitude*, I simply try to lay out an *aporia*, rather than a refutation" (TWB, 5).

[42] This is speculative idealism i.e. Hegel.

[43] Examples include the thought of death (AF, 59) or human extinction (AF, 57). As Gratton explains "Thinking the possibility of our impossibility, as Heidegger called death, then carries with it the seeds of the destruction of correlationism. In order to think oneself as mortal, one must consider one's death as not depending on a relation to one's thought. The correlationist cannot maintain a necessity to the correlation itself without defending idealism: if the relation was necessary, there would be no death, since one would always have to be *in relation to death* in order to actually die, which cannot be the case if one is *not*." Peter Gratton, "After the Subject: Meillassoux's Ontology of 'What May Be'," *Pli: The Warwick Journal of Philosophy* 20 (2009), 68.

[44] Readers might be reminded of Deleuze's radically empiricist "...plane of immanence." [Full quote: "When immanence is no longer immanent to something other than itself it is possible to speak of a plane of immanence. Such a plane is, perhaps, a radical empiricism." Gilles Deleuze, *Difference and Repetition* trans. Paul Patton (Athlone: Athlone Press, 1994), 47]. It is interesting to note that John Mullarkey interprets the Deleuzian position on immanence/radical empiricism as the "absolutization of immanence" in John Mullarkey, *Post-Continental Philosophy: An Outline* (Great Britain, Continuum, 2006), 13. This connection cannot be explored in detail here, but is clearly an interesting one.

[45] Gratton explains as follows: "Hence, correlationism must assert *positively* one unconditional, that is, absolute fact or condition: the facticity of contingency, and in particular, the contingency of the relation." Peter Gratton, "After the Subject: Meillassoux's Ontology of 'What May Be'," *Pli: The Warwick Journal of Philosophy* 20 (2009), 68.

[46] Gratton makes a similar point: "What we have, then, is a "hyper-chaos," since, as Meillassoux points out, without the principle of sufficient reason, not just every *thing* is contingent,

but so is every law. We must recall that *factialité* stipulates that every intra-worldly law is itself contingent and thus possible of being otherwise. For those looking to Meillassoux's return to rationalism as a means for eternally grounding the laws obtained in scientific analysis, Meillassoux's rational principle of "unreason" will surely disappoint." Peter Gratton, "After the Subject: Meillassoux's Ontology of 'What May Be'," *Pli: The Warwick Journal of Philosophy* 20 (2009), 71.

[47] Brassier is keen to point out that: "Meillassoux conducts his case against correlationism in a logical rather than empirical register..." in Ray Brassier, *Nihil Unbound: Enlightenment and Extinction* (London: Palgrave Macmillan, 2007), 58. Hägglund recognizes this when he tells us that Meillassoux's argument "...does not rely on an empiricist, positivist, or metaphysical discourse to attack transcendental philosophy. Rather, Meillassoux turns the central argument of transcendental philosophy against itself." Martin Hägglund, "The Challenge of Radical Atheism: A Response," *CR: The New Centennial Review* 9, no. 1, (2009), 241. That is Meillassoux allows the internal logic of transcendentalism to undermine itself.

[48] One should be careful to remember that Meillassoux is not claiming that reality is itself mathematical. Compared to Max Tegmark, Meillassoux's usage of mathematics is tame. Tegmark, operating on the assumption of a mind-independent reality, argues that the theory of everything (in physics), if it is ever achieved, will be articulated mathematically: "So here is the crux of my argument. If you believe in an external reality independent of humans, then you must also believe in what I call the mathematical universe hypothesis: that our physical reality is a mathematical structure. In other words, we all live in a gigantic mathematical object— one that is more elaborate than a dodecahedron, and probably also more complex than objects with intimidating names like Calabi-Yau manifolds, tensor bundles and Hilbert spaces, which appear in today's most advanced theories.

Everything in our world is purely mathematical – including you." Max Tegmark, "Shut up and calculate," http://arXiv:0709.4024v1 [physics.pop-ph], 2.

[49] The quote continues: "What Hume tells us is that *a priori*, which is to say from a purely logical point of view, any cause may actually produce any effect whatsoever, provided the latter is not contradictory. There can be no doubt that this is the evident lesson of reason, which is to say, of the thinking whose only fealty is to the requirements of logical intelligibility – reason inform us of the possibility that our billiard balls might frolic about in a thousand different ways (and many more) on the billiard table, without there being either a cause or a reason for this behaviour" (AF, 90). A further important point, and more evidence of Meillassoux's strict rationalism, is that "It is the senses that impose this belief in causality upon us, not thought. Thus, it would seem that a more judicious approach to the problem of the casual connection would begin on the basis of the evident falsity of this connection, rather than on the basis of its supposed truth. In any case, it is astonishing to note how in this matter, philosophers, who are generally the partisans of thought rather than of the senses , have opted overwhelmingly to trust their habitual perceptions, rather than the luminous clarity of intellection" (AF, 91).

[50] Or put differently a "determinate condition of chaos" (AF, 101, his italics).

[51] As Brassier notes "Cantor has shown that a bigger cardinality is always possible." Ray Brassier, *Nihil Unbound: Enlightenment and Extinction* (London: Palgrave Macmillan, 2007), 81.

[52] Brassier is again helpful here: "Thus at the logical level, possibility is governed by *contingency*, not *probability*." Ibid., 81.

[53] Brassier notes that "...he [Meillassoux] leaves the ontological status of stability entirely unclear." Ibid., 82.

b. The Transcendentalist Response III: Hägglund, Žižek, and Gabriel

[54] Hägglund does not only focus on the problem of succession, but also the remainder of Meillassoux's rejection of the principle of sufficient reason i.e. non-contradictory entities.

[55] Martin Hägglund, "The Challenge of Radical Atheism: A Response," *CR: The New Centennial Review* 9, no. 1, (2009), 242, his italics.

[56] This material precedes the correlation or what Hägglund more traditionally calls "the relation between thinking and being" Ibid., 242.

[57] Ibid., 242

[58] Martin Hägglund, "The Challenge of Radical Atheism: A Response," *CR: The New Centennial Review* 9, no. 1, (2009), 242, his italics.

[59] Ibid., 242.

[60] In their co-authored book that makes this case it is claimed that "...we are in need of a twenty-first-century post-Kantian Idealism..." Markus Gabriel and Slavoj *Žižek, Mythology, Madness, and Laughter: Subjectivity in German Idealism* (Great Britain: Continuum, 2009), 14.

[61] Ibid., 82, my italics.

[62] This is the problem of projection as Gratton puts it: "The correlationist, if he or she says anything, is attuned to the finite in the strict sense of saying to the believer what *cannot* be said about the *ansich*. That is to say, the correlationist shows the person of faith's dogmatism to be a 'projection' onto the 'in-itself', a projection perhaps worthy of analytic investigation, from Freud to Lacan and beyond, in terms of scope and power of these fantasies, but not as a compliment to their work." Peter Gratton, "After the Subject: Meillassoux's Ontology of 'What May Be'," *Pli: The Warwick Journal of Philosophy* 20 (2009), 65 his italics.

[63] Gabriel's principle problem with Meillassoux's metaphysics is that the only argument presented against anti-correlationism

is that it"...relies on the truth predicate in ancestral statements" Gabriel, op. cit., 86. For Gabriel Meillassoux has failed to engage the realism/antirealism debate that is properly at stake here and is not being fair to 'correlationism' when he restricts his undermining of it to ancestral statements alone.

[64] Adrian Johnston, *Badiou, Žižek, and Political Transformations: The Cadence of Change*, (Evanston: Northwestern University Press, 2009), 210.

[65] Ibid., 218, his italics.

[66] Contra Badiou Meillassoux is unlikely to find, as Žižek and Badiou have, the good in the re-actualization of Paulian universalism. See Slavoj Žižek, "The Politics of Truth, or, Alain Badiou as a Reader of St. Paul", in *The Ticklish Subject: The Absent Core of Political Ontology* (New York: Verso, 1999) and Alain Badiou, *St. Paul: The Foundation of Universalism*, trans. Ray Brassier (Stanford: Stanford University Press, 2003).

c. The Speculative Response: Gratton and Harman

[67] Gratton continues: "One can take this to be merely a strategy in *After Finitude* to strip correlationism of its agnosticism about reality and to take on directly the dominant attribute of contemporary philosophy. Nevertheless, while correlationism *assumes* the fact of contingency, it is also the case that Meillassoux's realism *speculates* from the fact—contingent and necessary, yes—of the phenomenal-noumenal split." Peter Gratton, "After the Subject: Meillassoux's Ontology of 'What May Be'," *Pli: The Warwick Journal of Philosophy* 20 (2009), 73.

[68] Ibid., 66.

[69] Gratton explains: "Speculative realism is founded on the principle that the in-itself has an *independent* existence and our knowledge of it extends to the necessity of its contingency, that is, that it *may or may not be*. We can't say *what it is*, what is 'universally given', but only hypothetically *what it would be* given contingent laws." Peter Gratton, "After the Subject: Meillassoux's

Ontology of 'What May Be'," *Pli: The Warwick Journal of Philosophy* 20 (2009), 5.

[70] Graham Harman, "On Vicarious Causation", *Collapse II: Speculative Realism* (London: Urbanomic, 2007) 172. Hereafter cited as VC.

[71] I will not be emphasizing it in my reading, but those with a broader interest in metaphysics will be happy to discover that that Harman defends 'substance' ontology: "Along with causation there is also the 'vicarious' part of the phrase, which indicates that relations never directly encounter the autonomous reality of their components. After thousands of years, 'substance' is still the best name for such reality. The widespread resistance to substance is nothing more than revulsion at certain inadequate models of substance, and such models can be replaced. Along with substance, the term 'objects' will be used to refer to autonomous realities of any kind, with the added advantage that this term also makes room for the temporary and artificial objects too often excluded from the ranks of substance" (VC, 173).

[72] This article is by no means representative of the core of Harman's thinking. Object oriented ontology is itself in a period of metamorphosis that makes a faithful reading almost impossible at this point. To date it is perhaps *Guerrilla Metaphysics* that best captures the framework of object oriented thinking. See Graham Harman, *Guerrilla Metaphysics: Phenomenology and the Carpentry of Things* (Chicago: Open Court, 2005).

[73] Despite moving past them Harman retains respect for the phenomenological tradition in relation to objects: "While the phenomenological movement of Husserl and Heidegger did too little to overcome the idealism of the previous cluster of great philosophers, they and their descendants often show a novel concern with specific, concrete entities. Mailboxes, hammers, cigarettes, and silk garments are at home in phenomenology in a way that was never true for the earlier classic figures of German thought. Even if Husserl and Heidegger remain too

attached to human being as the centerpiece of philosophy, both silently raise objects to the starring role, each in a different manner" (VC, 176).

74 Humans cannot, even if they so wish, exhaust the possibilities of the object. Harman's reasoning is that if humans do not exhaust objects then there is no reason to claim that objects exhaust *other objects*. The idea can be expressed as the claim that objects are not exhausted by their relations with other objects. For Harman objects are more than their *relations*. Objects shade or flit into momentary contact with other objects before withdrawing into the background once again.

75 The reader is advised to read through this short, but dense section for themselves (VC, 181-182). The proliferation of connections can be difficult to keep track of, but there is a sense that Harman recognizes that reality is likely to have this 'web-like' structure of interactions. Metaphysics should not be clear and concise in order to satisfy the human desire for clarity, but may require deference to the 'messiness' of the real.

76 As previously noted the metaphysical tone of Harman's essay takes some getting used to since it posits a number of complicated interactions but at this stage we have four objects: (A) real phenomenal whole (B) real I (C) sensual tree (D) real tree. According to Harman, object C cannot be conceptualized in its essence. It is "...encrusted with various sorts of noise" (VC, 182). He calls this *black noise* and it is his description of the various possible forms an object can take on in perceptual experience. There are three forms: (1) essential *structuring* qualities (2) accidental features (3) relations. There are then five possible relations that can occur: containment, contiguity, sincerity, connection, and "no relation" (VC, 183-4).

77 Metaphor is simply one way in which allure operates for humans: "For humans, metaphor is one such experience. When the poet writes 'my heart is a furnace,' the sensual object known as a heart captures vaguely defined furnace-qualities and draws

them haltingly into its orbit" (VC, 199).

[78] Heidegger comes very close to discussing the space of real objects in his treatment of the classic Aristotelian division between the mathematician and natural philosopher in book II of Aristotle's *Physics*. According to Heidegger Aristotle tells us that the natural philosopher is interested in natural bodies. She is interested in particular in self-motion as it is displayed in natural bodies. The mathematician, contra to the natural philosopher, is not only interested in natural bodies as they appear but in creating her own objects derived from natural bodies. The resulting objects of abstraction are the concepts of things or ideas. Heidegger turns the process of abstraction into a topological manoeuvre. Or more precisely he makes abstraction the act of de-placing. The inevitable separation that occurs in the process of abstraction is a withdrawing of something from place. Natural bodies always belong to a place: to be is to have a place. Whatever object is created after abstraction is without place. See Martin Heidegger, *Plato's Sophist* trans. Richard Rojcewicz and André Schuwer (Bloomington and Indianapolis: Indiana University Press, 2003), §15, 69-81.

Thinking 'le grand dehors'

a. 'Nature' and the Out-side

[79] Žižek has hinted at this idea throughout his work, but his most extensive engagement comes in Slavoj *Žižek "Unbehagen in der Natur. Ecology Against Nature," Bedeutung, 1, (2009).* Available online at:http://www.bedeutung.co.uk/index.php?option=com_content&view=article&id=10:zizek-unbehagen-in-der-natur&catid=6:contents&Itemid=16.

[80] Daniel B. Botkin, *Discordant Harmonies: A New Ecology for the 21st Century* (USA: Oxford University Press, 1992), 5.

[81] Jonathan Bate, *The Song of the Earth* (Cambridge, MA: Harvard University Press, 2002), 245.

[82] Ibid., 258.

[83] Bill Devall and George Sessions, *Deep Ecology: Living As if Nature Mattered* (Salt Lake City: Gibbs M. Smith Inc. 1985), 98.

[84] Ibid., 99.

[85] Timothy Morton, *Ecology Without Nature* (Cambridge: Harvard University Press, 2007).

[86] Or even *more* succinctly: "…'nature' does not exist…" In *Slavoj Žižek "Unbehagen in der Natur. Ecology Against Nature," Bedeutung, 1, (2009*), no pagination.

[87] In an interview with Glyn Daly, Žižek *is quite clear on this:* "What I am currently engaged with is the paradoxical idea that, from a strict evolutionary perspective, consciousness is a kind of mistake – a malfunction of evolution – and that out of this mistake a miracle emerged. That is to say, consciousness developed as an unintended by-product that acquired a kind of second-degree survivalist function. Basically, consciousness is not something which enables us to function better. On the contrary, I am more and more convinced that consciousness originates with something going terribly wrong…" Slavoj *Žižek* and Glyn Daly, *Conversations with Slavoj Žižek* (Cambridge: Polity, 2004), 59.

[88] Žižek, op. cit., no pagination.

[89] Jane Bennett, *Vibrant Matter: A Political Ecology of Things* (USA: Duke University Press, 2010), xi.

[90] Ibid., vii

[91] Ibid., x, her italics.

[92] Ibid., 3.

[93] Bennett puts it as follows: "...I will try, impossibly, to name the moment of independence (from subjectivity) possessed by things, a moment that must be there, since things do in fact affect other bodies, enhancing or weakening their power. I will shift from the language of epistemology to that of ontology, from a focus on an elusive recalcitrance hovering between immanence and transcendence (the absolute) to an active, earthy, not-quite-human capaciousness (vibrant matter)." Ibid., 3.

b. 'Wohin haben wir uns verirrt?'

[94] "...where have we strayed to?" is what Heidegger abruptly asks readers mid-way through his analysis. Martin Heidegger, "The Question Concerning Technology," *Basic Writings* Ed. David Krell (New York: HarperCollins Publishers, 1993), 318 and Martin Heidegger, *Vorträge und Aufsätze* (Frankfurt am Main: Vittorio Klostermann, 2000), 13. Hereafter cited as QCT followed by the English and then German pagination. I have cited the German text due to Heidegger's distinct reliance on the German language to evoke connections.

[95] In a sentence: "Technology is not equivalent to the essence of technology" ["*Die Technik ist nicht das gleiche wie das Wesen der Technik*"] (QCT, 311/7).

[96] The problem is rooted in the question. We still ask about essences in the manner of the ancients: 'what is a tree', 'what is a hammer' or 'what is technology?' The *form* of the question elicits a specific kind of response. Today we respond to the question 'what is technology' by answering that it is a "means to an end" and a "human activity" ["*ein Mittel für Zwekke*" "*ein Tun des Menschen*" (QCT, 312/7). These are the twin criteria of the instrumentalist definition.

[97] That is his discussion of 'revealing' [*das Entbergen*] and its association with the Greek *alētheia* [ἀλήθεια] in place of the Latinized truth of 'correctness' (*veritas*) allowing to provide the following definition of technology: "Technology is a way of revealing" ["*Die Technik ist eine Weise des Entbergens*"] (QCT, 318/13).

[98] This is the connection to bringing-forth (as with *poiēsis*) such that us the essence of technology "is something poetic" ["*ist etwas Poietisches*"] (QCT, 318/14).

[99] Heidegger wants to give *Gestell* a new meaning, contra the ordinary German understanding, as the essence of modern technology. His revised definition of the word Enframing is as follows: "Enframing means the gathering together of the setting-

upon that sets upon man, i.e., challenges him forth, to reveal the actual, in the mode of ordering, as standing-reserve" [*Ge-stell heißt das Versammelnde jenes Stellens, das den Menschen stellt, d.h. herausfordert, das Wirkliche in der Weise des Bestellens als Bestand zu Entbergen*"] (QCT 325/21). Enframing, once again through a linguistic connection, preserves other meanings. Through the word '*stellen*,' (the German for 'to set,' and here note that Heidegger introduces a hyphen between *Ge-* and *stell* to differentiate it from the ordinary sense of *Gestell*), Heidegger derives the senses of producing and presenting [*Her- und Dar-Stellen*]. These are related back to *poiēsis* as allowing what presences to be brought forward into unconcealment. Both Enframing and *poiēsis* are related as modes of revealing (*alētheia*).

100 How does this work? Enframing presents itself as permanent, or as an inevitable fate or destining.

101 On the issue of extending the human mind see Andy Clark, *Supersizing the Mind: Embodiment, Action, and Cognitive Extension* (Oxford, Oxford University Press, 2008).

102 Joseph Silk, *The Infinite Cosmos: Questions from the Frontiers of Cosmology* (Oxford: Oxford University Press, 2008), 112, my italics.

103 Stiegler's book draws heavily, in the stages we are considering upon both André Leroi-Gourhan and Gilbert Simondon, but I do not have time to consider their significant role here. The book, and the series that follows, is an ambitious attempt to draw metaphysics toward its external conditions especially on the point of subjectivity as contrastively illuminated against 'inert' technical objects. The book operates within the phenomenological method, in particular the ek-static temporal horizon introduced by Heidegger. Contra Heidegger Stiegler accepts the 'technical' future and attempts to understand our future according to it as an event. See Bernard Stiegler, *Technics and Time, 1: The Fault of Epimetheus* trans. Richard Beardsworth and George Collins (Stanford: Stanford University Press, 1998), 4-10.

[104] Ibid.,68.

[105] Bernard Stiegler, *Technics and Time, 1: The Fault of Epimetheus* trans. Richard Beardsworth and George Collins (Stanford: Stanford University Press, 1998), 21.

[106] Stiegler is, of course, aware of the reasons for this deficiency given the events of the twentieth century: "The twentieth century thereby appears properly and massively uprooting – and this will always provide the theme, in terms of alienation and decline, of the great discourses on technics." Ibid., 32

[107] Ibid., 21

[108] Ibid., 162.

[109] Ibid., 163.

[110] Ibid., 154. There is much more to Stiegler's argument than I have discussed here. The interplay between interior and exterior is discussed in relation to Derridean '*différance*' and arguably takes place against a much wider philosophical background that includes the Hegelian dialectical interplay between subject and substance.

[111] Just to confirm this recall Heidegger's famous views on the moon-landings: "...one can say that when the astronauts set foot on the moon, the moon *as* moon disappeared. It no longer rose or set. It is now a calculable parameter for the technological enterprise of humans." Martin Heidegger, *Four Seminars,* trans. Andrew Mitchell and François Raffoul (Bloomington: Indiana University Press, 2003), 38.

[112] Bernard Stiegler, *Technics and Time, 1: The Fault of Epimetheus* trans. Richard Beardsworth and George Collins (Stanford: Stanford University Press, 1998), 90. Such pessimism is shared by Slavoj Žižek:

[113] "There are at least four different versions of apocalyptism today: Christian fundamentalism, New Age spirituality, techno-digital post-humanism, and secular ecologism. Although they all share the basic notion that humanity is approaching a zero-point of radical transmutation, their respective ontologies differ

radically...New Age spirituality gives this transmutation a further twist, interpreting it as the shift from one mode of "cosmic awareness" to another (usually a shift from the modern dualist-mechanistic stance to one of holistic immersion). ...secular ecologism shares the naturalist stance of post-humanism, but gives it a negative twist-what lies ahead, the "omega point" we are approaching, is not a progression to a higher "post-human" level, but the catastrophic self-destruction of humanity." Slavoj Žižek *First as Tragedy, Then as Farce* (*London: Verso,* 2009), 94. On the problems of New Age spirituality, techno-digital post-humanism, and secular ecologism Heidegger is likely to have agreed: "...it is my conviction that a reversal can be prepared only in the same place in the world where the modern technological world originated, and that it cannot happen because of any takeover by Zen-Buddhism or any other Eastern experiences of the world" Martin Heidegger, "Only a God Can Save Us: *Der Spiegel's* Interview (September 23, 1966)," in *Philosophical and Political Writings: Martin Heidegger,* ed. Manfred Stassen. (New York: Continuum International Publishing Group, 2003), 44.

Hegel without Hope

[114] The quote continues: "But then, how do things emerge? Here I feel a kind of spontaneous affinity with quantum physics, where, you know, the idea there is that the universe is a void, but a kind of positively charged void – and then particular things appear when the balance of the void is disturbed. And I like this idea spontaneously very much...the fact that it's not just nothing; things are out there. It means something went terribly wrong, that what we call creation is a kind of cosmic imbalance, cosmic catastrophe, that things exist by mistake." Quoted in Adrian Johnston, *Žižek's Ontology: A Transcendental Materialist Theory of Subjectivity* (Illinois, Northwestern University Press, 2008), 195.

[115] See Fabio Gironi, "Science-laden theory: outlines of an unsettled alliance," *Speculations* 1 (2010).

[116] I am accepting the 'traditional' or conventional reading of Hegel as defended in recent years by Frederick Beiser, Robert Pippin, Stephen Houlgate and Robert Stern and to a certain extent Charles Taylor. Less conventional readings have started to appear in recent years including Brandon's important 'reconstruction' of Hegel (*Brandon's Hegel* as Robert Pippin puts it), but also the Hegel we have encountered earlier defended by Markus Gabriel and Slavoj *Žižek* (what I would call *Žižek's Hegel*). The debate is wide-ranging and beyond the scope of my remit. In my interpretation, a classical 'metaphysical Hegelian' one, Hegel is the thinker of Reason's necessary teleological 'coming-to-awareness' of itself. For the more traditional readings see Charles Taylor, Hegel (Cambridge: Cambridge University Press, 1975), Robert B. Pippin, *Hegel's Idealism: The Satisfactions of Self-Consciousness* (Cambridge: Cambridge University Press, 1989), Frederick Beiser, Hegel (New York/London: Routledge, 2005), Robert Stern, *Routledge Philosophy Guidebook to Hegel and the Phenomenology of Spirit (London: Routledge, 2002) and Stephen Houlgate, An Introduction to Hegel: Freedom, Truth and History* (Oxford: Blackwell, 2005). Brandom is expected to publish a monograph on Hegel in the near future, but Hegel is dealt with in both Robert B. Brandom, *Making it Explicit* (Cambridge, MA: Harvard University Press, 1994) and *Tales of the Mighty Dead: Historical Essays in the Metaphysics of Intentionality* (Cambridge, MA.: Harvard University Press, 2002). See also Robert B. Pippin, "Brandon's Hegel," European Journal of Philosophy 13, no. 3 (2005), 381-408. Gabriel and *Žižek* undertake the defence of their reading of Hegel in Markus Gabriel and Slavoj *Žižek, Mythology, Madness, and Laughter: Subjectivity in German Idealism* (Great Britain: Continuum, 2009). Regarding sublation the German word '*aufgehobener*' [*aufheben*] (sublated) has, as is well known, many meanings – to nullify, override, merge, repeal, cancel, abolished, reverse, raise or annul. We can find an example of its usage early in the *Phenomenology of Spirit*: "...this being-in-and-

for-itself is at first only for us, or *in itself*, it is spiritual Substance. It must also be this *for itself*, it must be the knowledge of the spiritual, and the knowledge of itself as Spirit i.e. it must be an *object* [*Gegenstand*] to itself, but just as immediately a sublated object, reflected into itself." *G.W.F. Hegel, Phenomenology of Spirit* trans. A. V. Miller (Oxford: Oxford University Press, 1977), 14. Hereafter cited as PS.

117 In Hegel's own words: "The only Thought which Philosophy brings with it to the contemplation of History, is the simple conception *of Reason*; that Reason is the Sovereign of the World; that the history of the world, therefore, presents us with a rational process" in G.W.F. Hegel, *Reading Hegel: The Introductions* ed. Aakash Singh and Rimina Mohapatra (Australia, Re.press, 2008), 116.

118 In his own words: "The more conventional opinion gets fixated on the antithesis of truth and falsity, the more it tends to expect a given philosophical system to be either accepted or contradicted; and hence it finds only acceptance or rejection. It does not comprehend the diversity of philosophical systems as the progressive unfolding of truth, but rather sees in it simple disagreements in (PS, 2)."

119 On this point Hegel claims that "The necessary progression and interconnection of the forms of the unreal consciousness will by itself bring to pass the completion of the series." (PS, 50)

120 Maurice Merleau-Ponty, *Phenomenology of Perception* trans: Colin Smith (London: Routledge, 2005), xviii.

121 *Alain Badiou, Theoretical Writings* trans. Ray Brassier (New York: Continuum, 2004), 22.

122 G.W.F. Hegel, *The Encyclopaedia Logic: Part 1 of the Encyclopaedia of Philosophical Sciences,* trans. T. F. Geraets, W. A. Suchting, and H. S. Harris (Indianapolis: Hackett, 1991), §212R.

123 In the sense that that Reason is in active progress toward a future: "What has just been said can also be expressed by saying that Reason is purposive activity [*Zweckmäßige Tun*]" (PS,12).

[124] On the role of infinity see Hegel's important claim that: "This simple infinity, or the absolute Notion, may be called the simply essence of life, the soul of the world, the universal blood, whose omnipresence is neither disturbed nor interrupted by any difference, but rather is itself every difference, as also their supersession; it pulsates within itself but does not move, inwardly vibrates, yet is at rest. It is self-*identical,* for the differences are tautological; they are differences that are none." (PS, 100).

[125] Braver notes that "Hegel argues that if we cannot know noumena, then there is no reason to call them real, and the world we experience simply becomes the world. What appears to us is not *mere* appearance but reality full stop, since we cannot talk about another realm which would supply the invidious contrast. Without a contrasting term, there should be no hesitation in calling the world we experience the real world, or even the really real (*ontos on*) world." Lee Braver, A *Thing of This World: A History of Continental Anti-Realism* (USA: Northwestern University Press, 2007), 85. This insight occurs at various points in the Phenomenology albeit in stages that are to be considered temporary: "Self-consciousness and being are the same essence...It is only the onesided, spurious idealism that lets this unity again come on the scene as consciousness, on one side, confronted by an *in-itself,* on the other. But...its essence is just this, to be immediately one and selfsame in *otherness,* or in absolute difference. The difference therefore *is,* but is perfectly transparent, and a difference that is at the same time none" (PS, 142). Hegel's attack centres on the thesis that there can be no in-itself that is not in-itself for us. For Hegel the act of thinking the in-itself sublates the in-itself in the order of self-consciousness: "Hence it comes to pass for consciousness that what it previously took to be the in-itself is not an in-itself, or that it was only an in-itself for consciousness" (PS, 54). Also: "Now, if we inquire into the truth of knowledge, it seems that we are asking what

knowledge is *in itself*. Yet in this inquiry knowledge is *our* object, something that exists *for us*; and the *in itself* that would supposedly result from it would rather be the being of knowledge *for us*" (PS, 53).

126 I am, of course, simplifying matters here and leaving aside the important role of negation in the dialectical process: "The disparity that exists in consciousness between the 'I' and the substance which is its object is the distinction between them, the *negative* in general. This can be regarded as the *defect* of both, though it is their soul, or that which moves them. That is why some of the ancients conceived the *void* as the principle of motion, for they right say the moving principle as the *negative*, though they did not as yet grasp that the negative is the self" (PS, 21, his italics).

127 In *Being and Nothingness* Sartre considers modern thought to be a triumph over Cartesianism. It has healed the rift between being and the appearances. In a nod to Hegel he tells us that we must not consider the appearances to be "inconsistent" reflections of true being. Rather we must come to accept that if an inconsistency appears this is just it, and nothing more besides. In Jean-Paul Sartre, *Being and Nothingness* trans. Hazel E. Barnes (London: Routledge, 1958), xxi. Sartre proceeds to unfetter the appearances from their negative connotations as non-being, illusion and error. In Hegelian style he discards the 'in-itself' behind appearances, but in my opinion he goes too far when he claims that what was once pure negativity (appearances) is now "full positivity" (Ibid., xxii). What Sartre has overlooked is that in removing this negative charge one loses the Hegelian nimbleness to prepare for the unexpected and what is not expected must remain negative. That it can become positive is something to hold out for, but it is not a characteristic of the appearances to be '*full positivity*.'

128 The moment of separation is not for Hegel itself negative although it has the 'negative' function of allowing the differenti-

ation that allows for development, self-movement, and self-positing since in order to self-posit one must begin a process of severance: "...what is thus *separated* [*Geschiedne*] and non-actual is an essential moment; for it is only because the concrete does divide itself, and make itself into something non-actual, that it is self-moving" (PS, 18). Schelling locates the singular impulse to philosophizing in the separation instigated on the part of free cognition between us and nature. This separation is achieved through reflection: "Reflection makes the separation between man and the world permanent by viewing the latter as a thing-in-itself, attainable neither by intuition nor imagination, neither by understanding nor reason." F.W.J. Schelling, "Ideas on a Philosophy of Nature as an Introduction to the Study of This Science," in *Philosophy of German Idealism: Fichte, Jacobi, and Schelling*, ed. Ernst Behler (New York: Continuum, 1986), 169.

[129] G.W.F. Hegel, *The Encyclopedia Logic: Part 1 of the Encyclopaedia of Philosophical Sciences*, trans. T. F. Geraets, W. A. Suchting, and H. S. Harris (Indianapolis: Hackett, 1991), §44.

[130] Here I am heavily indebted to Gironi's reading and many of these quotes are sourced from his important article 'Science-laden theory: outlines of an unsettled alliance.' See Fabio Gironi, "Science-laden theory: outlines of an unsettled alliance," *Speculations* 1 (2010).

[131] Ray Brassier, *Nihil Unbound: Enlightenment and Extinction* (London: Palgrave Macmillan, 2007), 228.

[132] Fox, Dominic. *Cold Wold: The Aesthetics of Dejection and the Politics of Militant Dysphoria* (Hants: Zero Books, 2009), 4

[133] I do not mean, of course, to confuse *Spirit* with God. I know that for Hegel *Spirit* is not a guiding hand or a theistic subject. I accept Nancy's powerful description of what is at work in Hegel: "The pure element of sense or of truth – what Hegel calls 'concept' or 'grasp' from the point of view of its activity and the 'idea' from the point of view of its presentation – is the element of 'spirit', which names infinite relation itself, the step

out of self into the other of all reality. This 'life of the spirit' is not something separate; it is not spirituality that floats above and beyond materiality. It is nothing – or simple abstraction – as long as it remains considered in itself as if it were outside the world of effectivity. It is the breath of spirit, but this breath is not immateriality: on the contrary, it is the unsettling of matter inseparable from matter itself, the sensible in so far as it senses, is sensed, and senses itself. It names the restlessness and awakening of the world, immanence always already tense, extended and distended within itself as well as outside itself; space and time, already, as the ex-position of every position." Jean-Luc Nancy, *Hegel: The Restlessness of the Negative* trans. Jason Smith and Steven Miller (Minneapolis: University of Minnesota Press, 2002), 19.

Contemporary culture has eliminated both the concept of the public and the figure of the intellectual. Former public spaces – both physical and cultural – are now either derelict or colonized by advertising. A cretinous anti-intellectualism presides, cheerled by expensively educated hacks in the pay of multinational corporations who reassure their bored readers that there is no need to rouse themselves from their interpassive stupor. The informal censorship internalized and propagated by the cultural workers of late capitalism generates a banal conformity that the propaganda chiefs of Stalinism could only ever have dreamt of imposing. Zer0 Books knows that another kind of discourse – intellectual without being academic, popular without being populist – is not only possible: it is already flourishing, in the regions beyond the striplit malls of so-called mass media and the neurotically bureaucratic halls of the academy. Zer0 is committed to the idea of publishing as a making public of the intellectual. It is convinced that in the unthinking, blandly consensual culture in which we live, critical and engaged theoretical reflection is more important than ever before.